INTERMEDIATE MODERN STU

INTERNATIONAL ISSUES

ST NINIAN'S H.S.
GIFFNOCK

ALLAN GRIEVE
and JOHN McTAGGART

Hodder & Stoughton

A MEMBER OF THE HODDER HEADLINE GROUP

The illustrations were drawn by: Hardlines Illustrations and Design; Richard Duszczak Cartoons.

The publishers would like to thank the following individuals, institutions and companies for permission to reproduce photographs in this book:

Action Plus (46); © AFP/CORBIS (53); © Assignments Photographers/CORBIS (32 top); Associated Press (15, 35, 67, 74, 96, 98, 117 bottom, 118, 122, 132, 136); © Bettman/CORBIS (31, 56, 93); © Charles O'Rear/CORBIS (112); © CORBIS (117 top); © David Turnley/CORBIS (115, 133); © Fotografia Inc./CORBIS (66); Life File (26 bottom, 27, 58 bottom); © Jack Fields/CORBIS (68); Life File/Emma Lee (26 top); Nigel Forster (82); © Peter Turnley/CORBIS (32 bottom, 34); PA News (21, 91); Sue Ford/Science Photo Library (88); © Stephanie Maze/CORBIS (58 top)

The publishers would also like to thank the following for permission to reproduce material in this book: BBC Scotland, *The Guardian*, *The Herald* and *Evening Times*, *Scotland on Sunday*, *The Scotsman*.

Every effort of has been made to trace ownership of copyright. The publishers will be happy to make arrangements with any copyright holder it has not been possible to contact.

Orders: please contact Bookpoint Ltd, 130 Milton Park, Abingdon, Oxon OX14 4SB. Telephone: (44) 01235 827720, Fax: (44) 01235 400454. Lines are open from 9.00–6.00, Monday to Saturday, with a 24 hour message answering service.

British Library Cataloguing in Publication Data
A catalogue record for this title is available from The British Library

ISBN 0 340 77987 X

Published by Hodder & Soughton Educational Scotland
First published 2000

Impression number	10	9	8	7	6	5	4	3	2
Year	2006	2005	2004	2003	2002				

Copyright © 2000 Allan Grieve and John McTaggart

Cover photo from Tom Van Sant/Geosphere Project/Science Photo Library
Typeset by Fakenham Photosetting Limited, Fakenham, Norfolk
Printed in Great Britain for Hodder & Stoughton Educational, a division of Hodder Headline Plc, 338 Euston Road, London NW1 3BH by J. W. Arrowsmith Ltd.

CONTENTS

INTRODUCTION

International Issues has been written to meet the needs of students taking Intermediate 1 and Intermediate 2 courses in Modern Studies. It can be used in association with support material published by the Higher Still Development Unit.

The book aims to provide students with the necessary knowledge and understanding to succeed at either Intermediate 1 or Intermediate 2 levels. There are activities which seek to develop the evaluating skills required by the course. Activities have been set up to challenge pupils at Intermediate 1 and Intermediate 2 levels. We believe that the teacher is best placed to know which activities are most appropriate for individual pupils.

The authors would like to thank the following individuals and organisations:

Clackmannanshire Council
German Tourist Board
NATO Information Office
European Commission Information Office
Embassies of China, South Africa and Brazil
Kathryn McEwan, Christine Little, Dave West and Ian Thomson (Auchmuty High School)
Numerous pupils of Auchmuty High School
Stephen Halder and Elisabeth Tribe at Hodder & Stoughton Educational.

Allan Grieve, Assistant Head Teacher, Falkirk High School
John McTaggart, Principal Teacher of Modern Studies, Boroughmuir High School

1 INTRODUCTION TO EUROPE

In this chapter you will learn about:
- different definitions of Europe
- background information on European countries
- definitions of nation, region and state
- different systems of government in Europe

There are many famous buildings across the whole of Europe

WHAT IS EUROPE?

Europe is one of the continents that make up the Earth's surface. Unlike the Americas or Africa, which are geographically and physically separate, Europe is linked by land to Asia, forming Eurasia. Europe consists of a large landmass with several offshore islands. The largest of these is Great Britain, made up of England, Scotland and Wales.

People in Britain have a different perspective on Europe compared to those who live 'on the Continent'. The very use of the phrase 'on the Continent' suggests that we in Britain regard ourselves as different, or separate from the rest of Europe. This perspective is sometimes described as an 'Anglocentric' viewpoint.

Defining Europe can be difficult. For example, Spain controls the Canary Islands and Madeira, and they are regarded as part of Spain for political and economic purposes. Many people who have visited these places may not realise that they are, in fact, located off the coast of North-West Africa, quite some distance from Spain itself.

Europe can be defined in both physical and political terms. In physical terms Europe extends from Britain and Ireland in the west to the Ural Mountains of Russia in the east, and from the Arctic Ocean in the north to the Mediterranean Sea in the south. This physical definition conflicts with a political definition. Russia extends for several thousand miles to the east of the Urals – should this part of Russia be included in a definition of Europe? Geographically that part of Russia is clearly in Asia, but politically it is governed from Moscow, which is quite clearly in Europe!

Some parts of Europe can be divided into regions. Scandinavia (Finland, Norway, Sweden and Denmark) is widely recognised as a 'unit' within Europe. Certainly, the first three countries – Sweden, Finland and Norway – form a discrete physical block, but Denmark is separated from them by sea and is linked to Germany.

Iberia is a recognisable area. The Iberian Peninsula comprises Spain and Portugal and is separated from the rest of Europe by the Pyrenees, on the Border with France.

The Low Countries, or Benelux, comprising Belgium, Netherlands and Luxembourg share many political ties.

The British Isles, made up of Great Britain, Ireland and the many smaller islands off the coast, are a geographical unit, but they are no longer a single political entity. Ireland became independent in the 1920s and has its own political system.

Other European 'regions' are more difficult to define. Central Europe, for example, contains Austria, Hungary and the Czech Republic. Wider definitions would also include Germany and Switzerland. 'The Balkans' is an area in southeastern Europe, but the precise definition varies according to the sources used.

Some descriptions of Europe are based on the political situation that existed from 1945 until 1989, when Europe was divided by the Iron Curtain. The man-made border that extended from the Baltic Sea to the Adriatic created an ideological divide. 'Western Europe' was democratic, capitalist and free. 'Eastern Europe' was undemocratic, Communist and enslaved. These terms survive at the end of the twentieth century, but the underlying ideological differences have been swept away.

The map of Europe has changed substantially in the late 1980s and 1990s. With the break-up of the former Soviet Union, old countries have been re-born and new countries have emerged. The 'Baltic States' of Latvia, Lithuania and Estonia have claimed independence for the first time in 50 years, whilst the likes of Ukraine and Belarus have gained independence for the first time in the modern era.

Czechoslovakia has broken into two countries, the Czech and Slovak Republics, in a peaceful process known as 'the Velvet Divorce'. Yugoslavia, on the other hand, has disintegrated after bloody and violent conflict.

The European Union is an organisation which represents 15 European states. But without doubt, Europe is larger than the borders of these countries – for example, Switzerland chooses not to be in the EU yet it is at the very heart of Europe.

Turkey is often considered to be part of Europe, yet geographically only a tiny part of the country is in Europe. Istanbul, located on the Bosporus, is regarded as 'the end of Europe', but politically the rest of the country is considered to be European. Geographically, the area is correctly known as Asia Minor.

The most meaningful definition of Europe is hard to find. To some people it might be the countries that compete in the European Football Championship – yet why does Israel compete?

ACTIVITIES

1 Using a blank map of Europe and an Atlas, mark on the following areas:

Russia Scandinavia Iberia
Low Countries British Isles
Central Europe Balkans
Asia Minor

2 'The map of Europe has changed substantially since the late 1980s.' Using the information above, give two pieces of evidence to support this statement.

Country	Capital City	Area (sq km)	Population (Millions)	Currency
Albania	Tirana	28 748	3.4	Lek
Andorra	Andorra-La-Vella	453	0.07	Franc and Peseta both used
Armenia	Yerevan	29 800	3.6	Dram
Austria	Vienna	83 859	8.1	Schilling
Azerbaijan	Baku	86 600	7.6	Manat
Belarus	Minsk	207 600	10.3	Rouble
Belgium	Brussels	30 519	10.2	Belgian Franc
Bosnia-Herzegovina	Sarajevo	51 129	3.6	Dinar
Bulgaria	Sofia	110 912	8.5	Lev
Croatia	Zagreb	88 117	4.5	Kuna
Cyprus	Nicosia	9 251	0.8	Cyprus Pound
Czech Republic	Prague	78 864	10.3	Koruna
Denmark	Copenhagen	43 094	5.2	Krone
Estonia	Tallinn	45 100	1.5	Kroon
Faroe Islands	Thorshaven	1399	0.05	Krone
Finland	Helsinki	338 145	5.1	Markka
France	Paris	551 500	58.3	Franc
Georgia	Tbilisi	69 700	5.4	Lari
Germany	Berlin	356 733	81.9	Mark
Gibraltar		6	0.003	Pound Sterling
Greece	Athens	131 990	10.5	Drachma
Hungary	Budapest	93 032	10.0	Forint
Iceland	Reykjavik	103 000	0.3	Krona
Ireland	Dublin	70 284	3.6	Punt
Italy	Rome	301 268	57.2	Lira
Latvia	Riga	64 600	2.5	Lats
Liechtenstein	Vaduz	160	0.03	Swiss Franc
Lithuania	Vilnius	65 200	3.7	Litas
Luxembourg	Luxembourg	2586	0.4	Luxembourg Franc
Macedonia FYR	Skopje	25 713	2.1	Dinar
Malta	Valletta	316	0.4	Maltese Lira
Moldova	Kishinev	33 700	4.4	Leu
Monaco	Monaco-Ville	1	0.03	French Franc
Netherlands	Amsterdam	40 844	15.6	Guilder
Norway	Oslo	323 877	4.3	Krone
Poland	Warsaw	323 250	38.6	Zloty
Portugal	Lisbon	91 982	9.8	Escudo
Romania	Bucharest	238 391	22.7	Leu
Russia	Moscow	17 075 400	148.1	Rouble
San Marino	San Marino	61	0.02	Lira
Slovakia	Bratislava	49 012	5.3	Koruna
Slovenia	Ljubljana	20 256	1.9	Tolar
Spain	Madrid	505 992	39.7	Peseta
Sweden	Stockholm	449 964	8.8	Krona
Switzerland	Berne	41 284	7.2	Swiss Franc
Turkey	Ankara	774 815	61.8	Turkish Lira
Ukraine	Kyev	603 700	51.6	Hryvna
United Kingdom	London	244 100	58.1	Pound Sterling
Vatican City		0.44	0.001	Lira
Yugoslavia	Belgrade	102 173	10.3	Dinar

ACTIVITIES

Study the previous information, then answer these questions.

1   Which three European countries are the largest in terms of population?
2   Which three European countries are the largest in terms of area?
3   In the European Champions League, the Preliminary Round draw produces the following games:

Olimpia Ljubljana	v	Paris St Germain
Ararat Yerevan	v	Vardar Skopje
Hertha Berlin	v	Partizan Belgrade
Slovan Bratislava	v	Ajax Amsterdam
Young Boys Berne	v	Legia Warsaw
HJK Helsinki	v	Dinamo Tirana
Valletta	v	Union Luxembourg

Which countries are involved in each of the games? Mark the cities involved on your blank map of Europe.

4   'The UK has a larger population than Germany. France and the UK have similar populations. Austria covers a larger area than the Czech Republic. Both Belgium and Belarus have over 10 million people.' Statement by Ruth Letters.

Give two reasons why Ruth Letters could be accused of exaggeration.

Map of Europe at the beginning of the twenty-first century

NATION, STATE OR REGION?

Within Europe the terms 'nation', 'state' and 'region' are often used. It is important to understand exactly what is meant by these words.

A state is an independent political unit. The United Kingdom is a state, but Scotland – despite having its own Parliament – is not a state. States are totally independent countries.

A nation is a group of people who share characteristics such as language, culture and history. Some nations are also states – they are known as 'nation states'. Germany is an example of a nation state. Other nations are clearly not states – Scotland is a nation, but it is not a state. Some of the various nations within the former Yugoslavia have fought for independence in the 1990s – Croatia, Bosnia-Herzegovina and Slovenia, for example, have become independent. Some nations exist across international frontiers. The Lapps are a national group, but they have no country of their own. Lapps live in Finland, Norway and in Sweden.

Regions can exist within countries, or across borders. Regions are difficult to define. Sometimes they are a geographical area bounded by natural features such as mountains or rivers. France is divided into regions on this basis – Normandy would be an example of such a region. Sometimes they are a political unit. In Germany there are several identifiable regions, most notably Bavaria in the southeast of the country.

SYSTEMS OF GOVERNMENT IN EUROPE

Since the fall of Communism in the late 1980s, all European states can claim to be parliamentary democracies. However, in some of the countries that used to be under Communist control, democracy is still in its infancy and people from Western Europe might not regard the systems as truly democratic.

ACTIVITIES

Match up the correct definitions for these terms. Write them out for yourselves.

Nation An independent political unit, with its own government.

State A geographical area bounded by rivers or mountains.

Region A group of people who share common language, culture and history.

In some parts of Europe, governments are unitary – they serve the whole country. France is an example of a unitary state where government is largely from Paris, with little power devolved to the regions. Germany, on the other hand, is a Federal Republic, where power is devolved to the regions. Each of the 16 Lander in Germany has decision-making power over a wide range of topics. Certain decisions are made by the Federal Government, now back in Berlin. The United Kingdom has a hybrid system. Scotland has a Parliament with considerable decision-making powers, and Wales has an Assembly with more limited powers. Northern Ireland was governed directly from London in the late 1990s, with plans for a Northern Ireland assembly held up due to continuing negotiations to end the Troubles.

FRANCE

France is a republic and a parliamentary democracy where power is shared between the President, the Government and Parliament. The people directly elect the President once every seven years. The President appoints the Prime Minister after each General Election. Parliament has two chambers – the National Assembly and the Senate. The people elect the National Assembly, while the Senate is chosen by a complex system involving the National Assembly, Local Councils and the regions. Government in France is centralised in Paris. The age for voting in France is 18. The French use a complicated proportional representation system, involving several rounds of voting.

GERMANY

The Federal Republic of Germany is a parliamentary democracy with a federal constitution. The Federal Government in Berlin deals with foreign affairs, defence, financial matters, customs, air transport and the postal service. There are two chambers of government. The Bundestag is the main legislative chamber and is directly elected. The Bundesrat is made up of people appointed by the regional governments. The regions, or Lander, have power over most policy areas and can pursue quite different policies from each other. Germany uses a voting system known as the Additional Member System, similar to that used for the Scottish Parliament. It combines elements of First Past The Post and Proportional Representation. Germans can vote from the age of 18.

NETHERLANDS

The Netherlands is a hereditary monarchy and parliamentary democracy. The powers of the royal family are mainly ceremonial. There are two chambers of government, the Eerste Kamer and the Tweede Kamer. Members of the Eerste Kamer are appointed by regional governments, while theTweede Kamer is elected by proportional representation. Limited powers are devolved to the regions. Dutch citizens can vote from the age of 18.

UNITED KINGDOM

The UK is a hereditary, constitutional monarchy and a parliamentary democracy. There are two chambers of government – the House of Commons and the House of Lords. The Commons is elected by a First Past The Post System. The House of Lords is made up of appointed members and hereditary peers. Attempts were underway in the late 1990s to reform the House of Lords. The Royal Family has ceremonial powers only. Scotland has a powerful law-making Parliament (established 1999), and Wales has a more limited Assembly. England has no elected assembly or parliament. UK citizens must be 18 before they can vote.

ACTIVITIES

Use the information provided about four European countries.

1 What is a monarchy?
2 Which of the six countries are monarchies?
3 What is a republic?
4 *'Throughout Europe people are allowed to vote from the age of 18.'* This is a statement by Gary Steen. Give evidence to show that Gary Steen is exaggerating.
5 What are the main differences between the systems of government in Germany and France. Mention at least three differences in your answer.

2

COMPARATIVE LIFESTYLES IN EUROPE

<table>
<tr><td>

In this chapter you will learn:
- the similarities and differences in lifestyle and living standards between communities in Scotland and other countries
- how to find out information about other communities in Europe

</td><td>

For Intermediate Modern Studies it is necessary to be able to make comparisons between the community in which you live, and at least one other community in another part of Europe (outside the UK).

</td></tr>
</table>

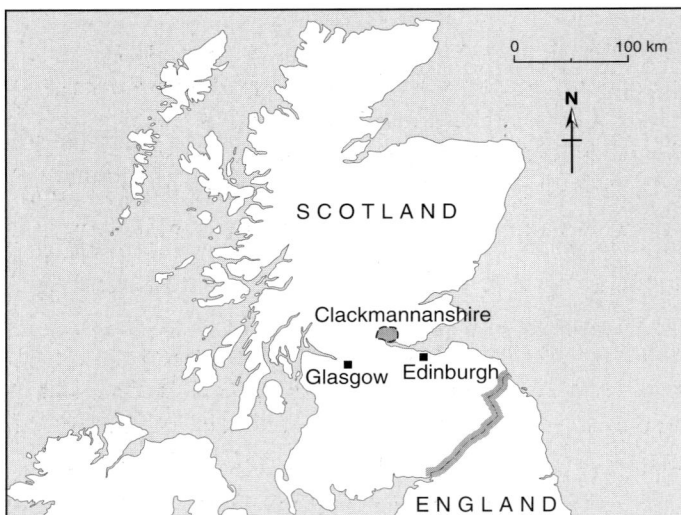

Clackmannanshire in Scotland

Forchheim in Germany

CASE STUDY

Case Study of a Scottish Community – Clackmannanshire

Location	Clackmannanshire is located in Central Scotland. To the north is the steep slope of the Ochil Hills and to the south is the River Forth. Clackmannanshire is the smallest local authority in Scotland, with a land area of just 15 662 hectares.
Population	48 850 people live in Clackmannanshire. Compared to other areas of Scotland Clackmannanshire has a comparatively young population – just 5.6% were aged 75 or over in 1993, compared to a Scottish average of 6.3%. There was an above average number of

0–14 year olds (20.1%) compared to a Scottish average of 19.0%. 89.9% of Clackmannanshire's people were born in Scotland, 7.8% in the rest of the UK and 2.3% outwith the UK.

Towns and Cities	Alloa is the largest town in Clackmannanshire with a population of just over 13 000. Along with Sauchie (to the east) and Tullibody (to the west), the total population is around 26 000 – more than half of the total for Clackmannanshire. Other towns of note are Tillicoultry, Alva, Menstrie, Dollar and Clackmannan – none of which have a population of more than 5000.
Employment	In the past large numbers of people were employed in coal mining. The coal mines have all closed down completely, but some open-cast coal mining is now carried out. This does not, however, employ very many people. Another traditional industry was brewing. Alloa once had more than a dozen breweries – now it has just one. In 1999 the largest brewery (one of the biggest in Britain) closed down. Associated with the brewing industry was the glass-making industry. Alloa Glass Works is the largest in Scotland and is now the biggest industrial employer in the town. Textiles are still important in Alloa and the smaller Hillfoots towns of Alva and Tillicoultry, but the numbers employed in this industry have also declined.
Education	Clackmannanshire has 20 primary schools and three large secondary schools – Alloa Academy, Lornshill Academy and Alva Academy. These schools are comprehensive schools – they serve a particular catchment area and take all the pupils from there. A small number of families choose to pay to send their children to private schools – Dollar Academy is the only private school in Clackmannanshire. There is also a Further Education College in Alloa, offering a limited range of courses. The nearest University is in Stirling, six miles away.
Leisure and Recreation	Alloa has an excellent leisure centre with a swimming pool and many other sports facilities. There is also a swimming pool in Alva and at Lornshill Academy. Golf is a popular sport, with six golf courses within the county, at Schawpark, Braehead, Muckhart, Dollar, Tillicoultry and Alva. Popular participation sports include fishing (at Gartmorn Dam) and bowling. The most popular spectator sport is football. The local team is called Alloa Athletic and they play in the Second Division of the Scottish League. They were established more than one hundred years ago.
Health	There is no proper hospital in Clackmannanshire. All accident and emergency cases and surgery is carried out in Stirling. There are local health centres in each of the towns and hospital facilities for elderly people.
Transport	There is no railway service to Clackmannanshire. The last trains ran in 1968, when the lines were closed. Local people have campaigned to get the line to Alloa re-opened, and this may happen soon. There are regular bus services from all the towns in Clackmannanshire to Alloa and to Stirling.

Agriculture	Farming is quite important in Clackmannanshire. Hill-sheep farming is found on the Ochil Hills, with dairy and arable farming elsewhere.
Problems	Crime is a growing problem in Clackmannanshire. Some of this is associated with drugs – housebreaking and robbery to finance drug-taking is common.
	Unemployment has hit the area hard with over 1000 jobs lost between 1998 and 2000. The Local Council has campaigned to get the government to invest money to attract new industries and businesses to come to Clackmannanshire.
Shopping	Alloa town centre has some shops, but many people prefer to travel to Stirling for shopping. The smaller towns have local shops. There are four large supermarkets in Alloa.
	At Tillicoultry there is a Designer Outlet Shopping Centre which attracts customers from all over Central Scotland.

Views of local people

'I like living in Clackmannanshire. It is in the middle of Scotland and ideal for getting to other places.'
– view of Hayley Mowatt

'Clackmannanshire is boring. There's nothing much to do. It doesn't even have a cinema or an ice rink.'
– view of Gemma Bain

'There's no job opportunities for young people – all the main employers have shut down. I want to move away as soon as I can.'
– view of Willie Fearns

ACTIVITIES

Look at the report on Clackmannanshire.
Using the same headings, compile a report about your home area. Your teacher may divide the class into groups for this exercise, with each group looking at particular headings.
Interview some members of your class and people from your family. Ask them what they think about the area in which they live.

CASE STUDY OF A GERMAN COMMUNITY – FORCHEIM

Location	Forcheim is located in Northern Bavaria, approximately 25 miles north of Nurnberg. It lies in an area known as 'Frankische Schweiz', or the 'Franconian Switzerland'. Forcheim is surrounded by wooded hills.
Population and History	30 000 people live in Forcheim. Forcheim was first mentioned in a document in the year 805, but it was probably founded between 550 and 600. In the Middle Ages it was a court of the Franconian kings and an important city of trade. Until the thirteenth century many German kings were crowned in Forcheim.

Districts	The Main-Danube Canal flows past Forcheim. The main town is to the east of the canal, with the suburbs (Stadtteil) of Buckenhofen, Burk and Forcheim-West on the opposite side. The nearest other town is Heroldsbach-Hausen, about 3 km from Forcheim.
Employment	Many people from Forcheim commute every day to the nearest large city – the Nurnberg/Erlangen conurbation. There is a large university at Erlangen and many of the staff there live in Forcheim. There is an industrial zone to the south of Forcheim with light manufacturing and electronics businesses.
Education	Forcheim has several secondary schools. As is the case throughout Bavaria, schools are selective. Gymnasiums are the top schools, where pupils usually go on to university. There are also Hauptschule and Realschule, which prepare pupils for work.
Leisure and Recreation	Like most German towns Forcheim has excellent sports facilities. There is an outdoor swimming pool that is open during the summer, and an indoor heated pool that is open in winter. Cycling and tennis are also popular participation sports. The main spectator sport is football. The local team is called Jahn Forcheim and they play in the Bavarian League – one of the Regionalised Fourth Divisions of the German Football Association.
Health	Forcheim has a large general hospital (Krankenhaus) which deals with most cases. There are numerous doctors and dentists, but they tend to operate from private consulting rooms rather than in health centres.
Transport	Forcheim is close to the main motorway (autobahn) from Coburg to Fussen. Forcheim is on a local railway line with regular services to Nurnberg and Bamberg. There are regular connections for services to the likes of Hamburg, Munich and Berlin.
Agriculture	Around Forcheim agriculture is important. Dairy herds supply milk for the town and its surrounding area. There are also many arable farms.
Problems	Forcheim is a relatively prosperous town with few serious problems. Unlike some other German towns there have been no real incidents of racism or right-wing extremism. Unemployment is low and crime rates are below the national average.
Shopping	Forcheim town centre has many small shops and local businesses. Germans often prefer to use old-fashioned bakers and butchers, rather than buying bread or meat from supermarkets. There are large supermarkets on the edge of the town. The nearest large shopping centre is in Nurnberg, which has one of the best shopping areas in Southern Germany.

Views of local people

'Forcheim is an ideal place to live. It has every amenity that a young person could want.'
– view of Gunter Schwarzenbeck

'*Forcheim is a bit quiet for my liking. I enjoy the night-life in bigger places nearby, like Erlangen and Nurnberg.*'
– view of Lisa Holzenbein
'*In Forcheim there are lots of opportunities to get well-paid jobs. I have no wish to ever move anywhere else.*'
– view of Helmut Muller
'*If you were retiring Forcheim would be a great place. I want to go to university and will move to one of Germany's big cities for that.*'
– view of Marina Schnellinger

ACTIVITIES

Writing a report – comparing your own community with another in Europe

Produce a report in which you compare your local community with another community elsewhere in Europe. You can use the same headings that have been included in the case studies of Clackmannanshire and Forcheim. Alternatively, you can add headings of your own. Remember that you should be comparing the two communities and drawing conclusions about the similarities and differences which you observe. Below are some ideas for choosing a community to compare with your own:

Does your school have a partner or exchange-school in another European country? If so it may be possible to exchange information with them. You may well find that they can communicate in English. You could always try out your skills in a foreign language! Many schools now have e-mail links to other schools throughout Europe. This means that you can exchange information very quickly. It is even possible to scan photographs and send them with e-mail.

Your town or local council may have a twin-town or council in another country. In fact, most Scottish local councils have several twin-towns. Forcheim, used as an example above,

Make use of the Internet to research information about other communities. Use a search engine and enter the name of a place in Europe. You may be surprised how many sites you find that have useful information. Examples of World Wide Web addresses for some communities are given below. A full list of the twin towns for Scottish towns and local councils can be found at:

http://www.cosla.gov.uk/euro/town_twinning_database_home_page.htm

Town	Scottish Twin Town	World Wide Web Address
Gomel (Belarus)	Aberdeen	http://gomel.lk.net/
Orleans (France)	Dundee	http://www.ville-orleans.fr/
Wurzburg (Germany)	Dundee	http://www.wuerzburg.de/
Watermael-Boitsfort (Belgium)	Annan	http://www.watermael-boitsfort.be/
Azkoitia (Spain)	Turriff	http://www.kz3.com/kz2000/azkoitia/index.htm
Korcula (Croatia)	Bute	http://www.korcula.net/default.htm
Aalborg (Denmark)	Edinburgh	http://www.eu-aalborg.dk
Munich (Germany)	Edinburgh	http://www.munich-tourist.de/english/m.htm
Albufeira (Portugal)	Dunfermline	http://www.portugal-info.net/algarve/albufeira.htm
Ingolstadt (Germany)	Kirkcaldy	http://www.ingolstadt.de/
Hersbruck (Germany)	Lossiemouth	http://staedte.seiten.de/hersbruck
Campi Bisenzio (Italy)	Monklands	http://www.nefer.com/campi/vivere/vivere.htm
Cognac (France)	Perth	http://www.cognac-france.com/
Ballerup (Denmark)	East Kilbride	
Seclin (france)	Larkhall	http://www.ville-seclin.fr/
Saint Germain en Laye (France)	Aye	http://www.ville-st-germain-en-laye.fr/
Schweinfurt (Germany)	Motherwell	
Turin (Italy)	Glasgow	www.commune.torino.it
Rosignano (Italy)	Musselburgh	

NB – Remember that website addresses often change. Some of these may have moved since publication.

is Stirling's twin-town in Germany. Stirling also has a twin-town in France – Villeneuve d'Ascq. Your local council may be able to give you information about their twin-towns, or they may be able to put you in touch with people who can help.

Have you visited somewhere on a school trip? If so then you may already have a pretty good idea what the town is like and how to get more information about it.

Is there somewhere that you have been to on holiday that you could compare with your own community? It is probably not a good idea to study a real tourist resort such as Benidorm or Salou, because they are not really typical of the countries they are in.

USEFUL INTERNET ADDRESSES – FOR FINDING OUT ABOUT COUNTRIES

The Lonely Planet series of travel guides have excellent web-sites about each European country. They can be found at:

http://travel.yahoo.com/Destinations/Europe//Countries/

You can then link with one click to lots of information about any European country that you choose.

By typing in the name of the country you are looking for in a search engine, you can easily find lots of resources that you may find useful. Be warned though; you may have to sift through many useless pages before finding exactly what you want! Other sites worth looking at include:

Austria

http://www.austria-cafe.com

Belgium

http://www.living-in-belgium.com/

http://belgium.fgov.be/

Denmark

http://www.skyt.com/Danmark/

http://rt66.com/~korteng/da.htm

Finland

http://virtual.finland.fi/

http://www.publiscan.fi/

France

http://www.ambafrance.org.uk

http://focusmm.com.au/france/fr_anamn.htm

Germany

http://www.german-embassy.org.uk

Greece

http://www.areianet.gr/infoxenios

http://www.greekembassy.org/

Ireland

http://www.virtualireland.com/

http://ireland.iol.ie/tip/

Italy

http://www.mi.cnr.it/WOI/woiindex.html

http://www.italyemb.org/

Luxembourg

http://www.luxembourg.co.uk

Netherlands

http://www.VisitHolland.com

http://www.netherlands-embassy.org/

Portugal

http://www.portugal-info.net/

http://www.portugal-web.com/

Spain

http://www.sispain.org/

http://www.spainemb.org/information/indexin.htm

Sweden

http://www.webcom.com/sis/

http://www.swedenemb.org/

Social and Economic Statistics For Selected European Countries

Country	Infant Mortality Rate (per 1000 live births)	Life expectancy at birth	Primary pupil/ teacher ratio	TVs per 1000 people	GNP per capita ($)	GNP per capita, annual growth, 1995/6
Austria	5	77	12	480	28 110	1.0
Belgium	6	77	12	460	26 440	1.4
Bulgaria	16	71	17	260	1190	−8.8
Croatia	10	72	20	230	3800	4.7
Czech Republic	6	73	20	380	4740	4.6
Denmark	6	75	10	540	32 100	1.8
Estonia	13	69	17	360	3080	5.2
Finland	4	76	11	500	23 240	3.5
France	5	79	19	580	26 270	1.0
Germany	5	76	18	550	28 870	0.9
Greece	8	78	16	210	8210	1.2
Hungary	11	69	11	520	4340	2.6
Ireland	6	76	23	320	17 110	8.7
Italy	6	78	11	430	19 880	0.7
Latvia	16	68	14	470	2300	3.5
Luxembourg	7	76	15	490	41 210	1.0
Moldova	26	68	23	280	590	−2.7
Netherlands	5	78	19	490	25 940	3.9
Norway	5	77	9	430	34 510	4.6
Poland	12	71	16	300	3230	6.2
Portugal	7	75	12	230	10 160	2.4
Romania	21	70	20	200	1600	4.7
Russia	20	65	20	380	2410	−5.0
Slovakia	10	71	24	280	3410	6.3
Spain	5	78	18	430	14 350	1.6
Sweden	4	78	11	470	25 710	0.8
Switzerland	5	78	12	400	44 350	−1.2
Turkey	41	68	28	270	2830	5.0
Ukraine	18	69	20	230	1200	−8.5
United Kingdom	6	77	16	780	28 020	1.4
Yugoslav Federation	19	72	22	300	1400	1.8

3

SOCIAL AND ECONOMIC ISSUES IN EUROPE

In this chapter you will learn about:
◆ the origins and development of the European Union
◆ decision-making processes in the European Union
◆ current and future issues for the European Union
◆ the European Single Currency
◆ European Union Regional policies
◆ the Common Agricultural Policy
◆ the Common Fisheries Policy

Map of Europe after World War Two

THE ORIGINS OF THE EUROPEAN UNION

World War Two caused widespread death and destruction in Europe. The United Kingdom suffered bomb damage, but much of mainland Europe saw bombing and fighting on a much greater scale. The infrastructure of Europe – roads, railways, power supplies and communications – were largely destroyed by the War.

The end of the War also caused large-scale movements of people. Europe's borders were re-drawn. Poland, for example, although it continued to exist, was moved westwards. Substantial areas were lost to the Soviet Union, but territory was gained from Germany. Germans who lived in the area that was now Polish were displaced, and settlers from the areas lost in the east moved in.

Twice in the twentieth century Europe had been drawn into massive warfare. The major powers of the time were determined that this should not happen again. One of the main reasons for the rise of Hitler and German aggression in the 1930s had been the fact that Germany was punished and economically crippled for its part in starting World War One. The UK, USA and the other allied powers were determined that this situation should not arise again. Consequently they invested huge amounts of money to rebuild Germany, trying to ensure that democracy would have a chance to take root in a stable economic climate.

Europe was devastated by World War Two

Two French politicians, Jean Monet and Robert Schuman, proposed that European countries should sign a treaty to bring their economies closer together. They had a vision that if European countries depended upon each other economically then they could never afford to go to war with each other. As a result, in 1951 the European Coal and Steel Community (ECSC) was established, and France, Belgium, Italy, Netherlands, Luxembourg and Germany signed the Treaty of Paris. The inclusion of both France and Germany was significant, as they were the two most powerful forces in mainland Europe at the time.

The ECSC was a success and the six member countries decided to expand the organisation to cover other sectors of the economy. In 1957 they signed the Treaty of Rome to create the European Economic Community (EEC), which was also known as the Common Market. The process of expanding the remit of the organisation is known as 'deepening'.

The success of the EEC encouraged other countries to want to join. They were attracted by the Common Market principle – there were to be no barriers to trade between member countries, and a Common External Tariff would be applied to goods coming into the community. The purpose of this was to protect European industries from competition from other parts of the world, and to give them a wider market than just their own country. Britain first tried to join the EEC in the early 1960s but France was opposed to British membership at that time. Britain tried again in 1967, but was again blocked by France. They felt that Britain had strong links with the USA and the Commonwealth, which would go against the principles of the EEC.

Britain, Ireland and Denmark eventually did join in 1973. The process of more countries joining is known as 'widening'. The membership rose to ten in 1981 with the addition of Greece, and then to 12 in 1986 when Spain and Portugal were admitted.

By late 1992, as a result of the Maastricht Treaty, the organisation was known as the European Union. Deepening meant that the EU affected almost every aspect of life in member countries. The Maastricht Treaty gave the go-ahead for the development of a single European Currency, which was partly introduced in 1999. The Maastricht Treaty also established the Committee of the Regions, which is designed to give a voice to regional governments in Europe. Many of the EU countries are large, and it would be unfair for one central government to speak on behalf of all the people. Scotland is represented on the Committee of the Regions. The most important aspect of Maastricht was probably the Social Charter, which established European-wide standards for the protection of workers' rights, working conditions and equal opportunities. The Conservative government of the time was fiercely opposed to this, and Britain initially 'opted out' of this part of the Maastricht Treaty. However, following the election of the Labour government in 1997 Britain adopted most of the principles of the Charter.

In January 1993 the Single Market was created. All goods could now be exchanged within the EU without any delay at frontiers. People also found it easier to move around the member states of the European Union. Border controls were ended, and people had equal access to education, employment and benefit rights throughout the European Union.

Membership grew to 15 countries in 1995 when Austria, Finland and Sweden were added to the EU. The organisation is unlikely to widen further until the twenty-first century when a number of former Communist countries of Central and Eastern Europe are likely to join.

TIME-LINE FOR THE DEVELOPMENT OF THE EUROPEAN UNION

1945	End of World War Two
1951	European Coal and Steel Community formed Treaty of Paris
1957	European Economic Community (EEC) set-up. Six original members – France, Belgium, Netherlands, Luxembourg, Italy, Germany
1963	Britain applies to join – rejected by France
1967	Britain again applies to join – again rejected by France
1973	Six become nine – Britain, Ireland and Denmark join the EEC
1981	Nine become ten – Greece joins the EEC
1986	Ten become twelve – Spain and Portugal join the EEC
1992	Treaty of Maastricht
1993	Single European Market comes into operation European Union formed
1995	Twelve become fifteen – Austria, Finland and Sweden join the EU
1999	Single European Currency comes into operation (Britain chooses not to join)

DECISION-MAKING IN THE EUROPEAN UNION

Those who oppose Britain's membership of the EU often claim that 'decisions are made in Brussels' and are 'outwith Britain's control'. This is not the case. There is no 'European Government' in Brussels or anywhere else – decisions are made by a Council of Ministers.

The Council of Ministers is made up of Government Ministers from all the member states. Depending on what is on the agenda for a meeting of the Council, countries will send an appropriate Minister. Sometimes, for a summit meeting, each country will send its Prime Minister.

ACTIVITIES

1 What were the main consequences of World War Two?

2 Why were Jean Monet and Robert Schuman important in the growth of European unity?

3 What was the aim of the European Coal and Steel Community?

4 Name the six countries that signed the Treaty of Rome in 1957.

5 What was the principle of the Common Market?

6 Why was Britain refused entry to the EEC in the 1960s?

7 Which countries joined the EEC in 1973?

8 What is meant by 'widening'?

9 What is meant by 'deepening'?

10 What were the main features of the 1992 Maastricht Treaty?

11 What is the Single Market?

12 Which countries joined the EU in 1995?

13 *'Britain has always been in favour of every part of the European Union'* – statement by Dean Milligan
Why can Dean Milligan be accused of exaggeration?

ACTIVITIES

Make your own notes on the role of each of the following:

◆ The Council of Ministers
◆ The European Commission
◆ The European Parliament

The European Commission is the civil service of the European Union. There are 20 European Commissioners, each of whom has a remit for a particular policy area. The full-time officials, or Eurocrats as they are sometimes called, can suggest new laws but they do not make them. One of Britain's Commissioners is the former Labour Party leader Neil Kinnock, who is responsible for transport.

The European Parliament, which meets in Strasbourg, looks at proposals put forward by the European Commission. It is made up of over 600 directly elected Members, but has little power over policy in the member states. The Parliament does influence the budget of the European Union, and has the power to dismiss the European Commission.

Certain European laws need to be translated into national law in each member parliament, including Westminster.

CASE STUDY

The European Commission

In early 1999 accusations of fraud and mismanagement were levelled at the heart of the European Union. A Commission official released information to the European Parliament, which highlighted cases of fraud. Paul Van Buitenen identified 'incompetence and unwillingness of the administration to deal efficiently with fraud and irregularities.'

The Commission – the civil service of the EU – is run by a group of 20 Commissioners, under the leadership of the European Commission President. In March 1999 the then President, Jacques Santer, issued an ultimatum to the European Parliament – 'back us, or sack us'.

The European Parliament cannot force individual commissioners to resign or sack them. They can, however, sack the entire European Commission en masse. In the event it did not come to this. When an independent report was published, backing up the allegations of fraud and mismanagement, the commissioners decided to resign en masse. Certain commissioners were named in person in the report – most significantly Jacques Santer and Edith Cresson (former Prime Minister of France) – but others such as Britain's Neil Kinnock were cleared of any wrongdoing.

The accusations included the fact that commissioners were guilty of finding jobs for their friends and family, awarding contracts to businesses of friends and family, and wasting taxpayer's money.

The organisation of the EU is such that it cannot function properly without commissioners. It was therefore necessary to appoint a new group of commissioners as quickly as possibly. Obviously Santer would be unable to continue as President, and moves began to find a replacement. The candidate who proved to be acceptable to the European Parliament was former Italian Prime Minister Romano Prodi. In September 1999 he appointed his new team of European Commissioners and began the task of rebuilding confidence in the Commission.

ACTIVITIES

Read the Case Study of the European Commission and answer the questions which follow.

1 Why were the European Commission criticised in 1999?
2 What forced the entire European Commission to resign?
3 Which Commissioners came in for the most criticism?
4 Who took over as the new President of the European Commission?
5 'The European Parliament has total power over the Commission.'
– view of Alison Hutchison
Do you agree with this statement? Give evidence to support your answer.

ACTIVITIES

1 Why is the year 2002 significant for the Euro?
2 Why does the EU need to have its own military policy?
3 What is the Democratic Deficit?
4 'It is clear what changes need to be made to the CAP.'
– statement by Simon Christopher
Why is Simon Christopher guilty of exaggerating?
5 What is meant by 'Richer members effectively subsidise the poorer members'?

The economic ties between European countries are becoming stronger and stronger

THE EUROPEAN UNION IN THE TWENTY-FIRST CENTURY

The main goals for the first part of the new millennium are:
- to fully implement the Single European Currency (EURO)
- to develop a common foreign and security policy
- to enlarge the community with new members
- to address the Democratic Deficit
- further reform of the Common Agricultural Policy
- reform of the EU Budget system

The Euro was introduced for business transactions in 11 member states (known as Euroland) in January 1999. The Euro should replace individual currencies across Euroland in 2002. The EU hopes that more countries will join.

The Kosovo conflict showed that Europe has different military objectives to the USA. Increasingly the EU will need to have its own foreign and military policy, independent of NATO and the USA.

Many countries from Eastern and Central Europe are keen to join the EU. This would bring difficulties, but the EU is beginning the process of allowing new members to join.

The European Parliament is the only directly elected part of the EU, yet it is the least powerful part. This is known as the Democratic Deficit. The powers of the Parliament are being increased. The mass resignation of the European Commissioners was an example of the European Parliament using its power.

There is agreement that the Common Agricultural Policy needs to be reformed, but no agreement on exactly what changes are necessary.

The EU is paid for by member states. Some of the richer members feel that they now pay in too much, and effectively subsidise the poorer members. Britain negotiated a reduction in payments in 1984, and other countries like Germany feel that this should be reviewed.

THE TREATY OF AMSTERDAM

Every five years the EU holds a major summit meeting at which the objectives for the future are identified. In 1992 this meeting took place in Maastricht, and in 1997 it was held in Amsterdam.

The Treaty of Amsterdam had four main objectives:
- to place employment and citizens' rights at the heart of the Union
- to sweep away the last remaining obstacles to freedom of movement and to strengthen security
- to give Europe a stronger voice in world affairs
- to make the Union's institutional structure more efficient with a view to enlarging the Union, with new Member States joining.

In other words, the Treaty of Amsterdam consolidates each of the three great 'pillars' which have been the foundation for the Union's work since the Maastricht Treaty of 1 November 1993: the European Communities (first pillar); the common foreign and security policy (second pillar); and co-operation in the fields of justice and home affairs (third pillar).

EU budget agreed

European Union leaders have reached agreement on a reform of the organisation's 85bn Euro (£60bn) budget. It took the political leaders, meeting in Berlin, 20 hours of talks before they managed to reach a compromise. The new budget guidelines cover the period from 1999 until 2006, and pave the way for new members to join the European Union. These include Poland, Hungary, the Czech Republic and Cyprus.

The UK Foreign minister Robin Cook said the deal meant that the EU could afford to take in poorer countries from Eastern Europe. A Polish spokeswoman said her government was 'delighted' at the outcome. The mixture of compromises reached reflects differing national priorities. France stood by its farmers, Spain defended its development aid while the UK refused to leave without keeping its special budget rebate.

The agreement cuts farm subsidies that take up 42% of the EU's annual budget, although not by as much as many had hoped. It also reallocates spending on poor regions.

The agreement includes a new method of calculating contributions to the EU budget. Currently every country sends a proportion of its VAT revenue to Brussels. By 2004 budget contributions will be based on a proportion of Gross National Product.

The union's richer countries, Germany, the Netherlands, Austria and Sweden, had hoped for cuts in their budget contributions, but all they got were slight reductions. Germany, for example, wanted a reduction in its net payment of 3.5bn Euros ($3.8bn). Officials said it ended up with a cut of only 700m Euros ($760m). The United Kingdom, meanwhile, managed to keep its special rebate – now worth around 3.5bn Euros (£2.33bn or $3.8bn) – which was originally agreed in 1984. 'Our net contribution remains as it is,' said Prime Minister Tony Blair. 'Not a Euro more, not a Euro less.'

Germany's Chancellor Gerhard Schröder admitted that Germany had failed to push through its demands. The French Prime Minister Lionel Jospin called the breakthrough 'a good moment for Europe'. Belgian's Finance Minister Jean-Jacques Viseur, spoke of a 'good agreement'.

ACTIVITY

'The UK, Germany and Spain all receive more in payments from the EU than they put in.'
– view of Richard Cook
What evidence is there that Richard Cook is making selective use of facts?

Who benefits from the EU?

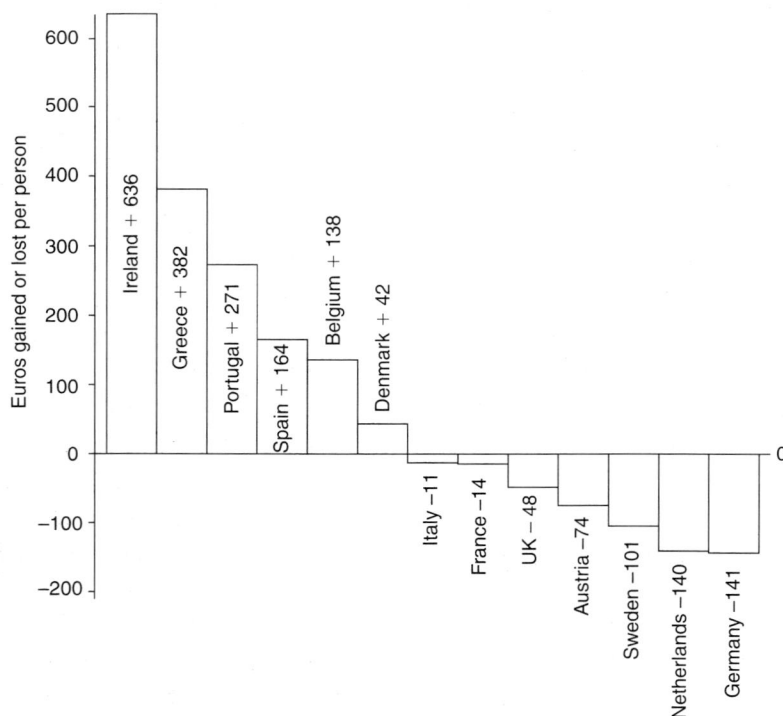

Euros gained or lost per person

- Ireland + 636
- Greece + 382
- Portugal + 271
- Spain + 164
- Belgium + 138
- Denmark + 42
- Italy –11
- France –14
- UK – 48
- Austria –74
- Sweden –101
- Netherlands –140
- Germany –141

(Yearly Payment Per Person in Euros)

The new Euro

ACTIVITIES

1 What were the four main objectives of the Treaty of Amsterdam?

2 How much is the total EU budget worth?

3 According to Robin Cook, what will the budget deal mean that the EU can do?

4 How is the value of each country's contribution calculated at present?

5 How will it be calculated in future?

6 *'Germany will be unhappy with the outcome of this deal'.*
   – view of Sarah Brand
   What evidence is there to support Sarah Brand's view?

7 *'Britain managed to keep its special budget rebate. The French Prime Minister was pleased with the deal, but the Belgian Finance Minister was not happy.'*
   – statement by James Baird
   Give evidence to show that James Baird is exaggerating.

THE SINGLE EUROPEAN CURRENCY (THE EURO)

On January 1st 1999 the Euro was launched. The eurozone, or 'Euroland' as it is known, is made up of 11 members:

Austria	Italy
Belgium	Luxembourg
Finland	Netherlands
France	Spain
Germany	Portugal
Ireland	

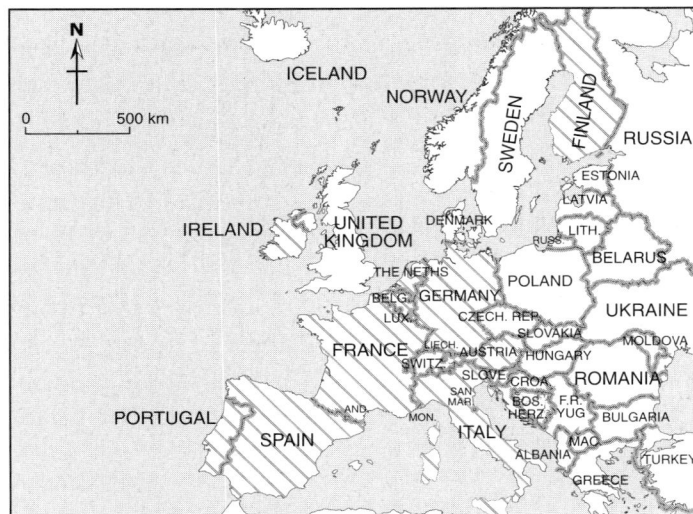

Map of Euroland

290 million people live in Euroland, more than in the whole of the United States of America. Together the Euroland countries have a Gross Domestic Product of $6480 billion – slightly smaller than that of the USA.

Only four EU countries did not join Euroland – Denmark, Sweden and the UK chose to stay out, while Greece wanted to join but failed to meet the economic conditions necessary.

From 1999 all business transactions in Euroland are being carried out in Euros. Although people will continue to use their own coins and notes until 2002, they are really using Euros with a conversion-rate to translate prices into their own currencies.

There are 100 cents in each Euro, but calculating the value of the Euro on the financial markets proved to be much more difficult. When the Euro was introduced the exchange rate was set against international currencies. After January 1999 the value of the Euro fell throughout most of the next year, indicating that the value had been set too high. Some critics of the Euro said that the whole system was doomed to failure.

TIMETABLE FOR THE EURO

January 1st 1999 The exchange rates of all currencies in Euro countries were fixed and the Euro became a currency in its own right. Euroland citizens could open bank accounts, and make transactions in Euros, but were not obliged to do so.

January 2002 Euro coins and banknotes introduced. Some countries are planning a two-month transition period where both old currencies and the new Euros would be legal tender.

July 1st 2002 All national coins and banknotes withdrawn and only Euros and Cents to be legal tender in Euroland.

THE IMPACT OF THE EURO

Bankers and accountants were first to see the impact of the Euro. From January 1999 most banks, all stock markets and many companies did their transactions and accounts in Euros. Even companies in Britain, outside of Euroland, found that it was necessary to use Euros when dealing with businesses in countries that had joined the system.

Shoppers in Euroland found that there were two prices on the labels of goods – one in Euros and one in their national currency. British people going on holiday in Euroland will find that they have to convert their pounds into Euros – but if they are visiting several Euro countries then they will not have to make any further changes. This will save them money on commission charges at travel agents or at the bureaux de change. Obviously, a German going on holiday to Spain or Portugal will not have to change their currency in future.

RULES FOR JOINING THE EURO

The rules for joining the Euro currency are strict. If the UK wants to join at some point in the future, then it must meet the following criteria:
Inflation should be within 1.5% of the Eurozone
Exchange rate should be stable in relation to the Euro
Annual budget deficit should be below 3% of their Gross Domestic Product
Public Sector debt (the total amount of money owed by the government) must be less than 60% of GDP.

EUROPEAN CENTRAL BANK

The European Central Bank (ECB) sets monetary policy for all the members of Euroland. The new bank is modelled on Germany's Bundesbank. It is independent from political influence and can set interest rates at whatever level it feels is appropriate.

The ECB's key tasks are to:
- Decide monetary policy, such as setting interest rates.
- Maintain price stability.
- Support economic policies of member states as long as they do not affect inflation rates.
- Conduct foreign exchange operations with countries outwith Euroland.
- Promote smooth operation of payment systems that link banks.

The ECB is based in Frankfurt, Germany.

SHOULD BRITAIN JOIN THE EURO?

Membership of the Euro has been a political issue in Britain since the mid 1990s. The leaders of the Conservative Party have been consistently opposed to membership, although there are people in the party who disagree. Michael Hesseltine and Kenneth Clarke, both prominent figures in the Conservative Party, have been long-term supporters of closer European integration.

When Tony Blair's Labour Party won the 1997 General Election, their policy towards the Euro was one of caution. Blair said that Britain would support the Euro in the long-term, but that he would only take the country in after a referendum of the British people. This 'wait and see' policy seemed to be popular with the voters. The Conservatives have been more outspoken in their opposition to joining the Euro.

In February 1999 an opinion poll was carried out to gauge public reaction to the Euro. The results are illustrated in the pie chart.

Some of the comments people made included:

For

'*How can we have a truly common market without a common currency and a common language? For the former, the Euro is the best solution so far proposed. For the latter, I propose Esperanto. The only people who benefit from the current lack of commonality are currency speculators and translators.*'
Natalie Davie

'*The economic benefits in terms of stability and trade are many. Similarly, the social benefits to the citizen far outweigh any perceived erosion of sovereignty.*'
Richard Shields

'*The business world is already going to be dealing the Euro and if Britain does not join, it will cause economic problems, job losses and much more. For once Britain needs to look to the future instead of living in the past. Who needs to have the Queen's head in their pocket?*'
Fiona Grubb

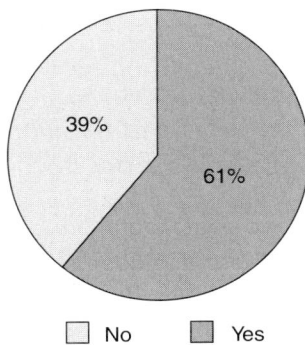

39%

61%

☐ No   ◼ Yes

Should Britain join the Euro?

'It would be a big blunder not to join the Euro now, since ultimately Britain will have to join!'
Robbie Gannon

'If the UK fails to join Europe, then inevitably big businesses will decide to relocate to Europe, with its stronger and more stable economic position! Britain must join!!!'
Sarah-Jane Marrs

'Dump the pound now! Federal Europe is the way to go.'
Brendan Knight

'As I understand it, it would take Britain three years to join from the point of saying yes. The fact that joining the Euro would cut thousands off my mortgage and other credit interest payments is sufficient incentive for me.'
Melanie Gray

Against

'The Euro will prevent us from taking economic decisions in our interest. If there is a recession in the UK we will be at the whim of bankers in Frankfurt as to whether we can recover from it.'
Kerry Smith

'I am firmly opposed to joining the Euro until we see whether it works over the next two or three years. However, I have been panicked into voting "Yes" by the suggestion that we should join our "natural" partners, the US. Anything, anything is preferable to that.'
James Thomson

'Britain became Great because of it's "not part of Europe" mentality. Continentals (France and Germany spring to mind most readily) have botched up the history of Europe for centuries. Why should we expect anything different? Let's not get tied up with them. I'm tempted to suggest we should even pull out of the EU altogether. What a load of cobblers.'
Gemma Halley

'Please, no. The Euro would be terrible for us. Any meagre voice that we still have would be totally lost. The UK is already small enough and growing smaller, why help larger countries to engulf us? Personally, I'm voting NO in the referendum.'
Michael Taylor

'The time will never be right for the Euro in Britain because we value our independence and freedom. We should never join the Euro, we don't need it.'
Gayle Stevenson

Write a detailed report on the implementation of the Euro.

Use the following headings:

- What is Euroland? (50 words approximately.)
- Timetable for the Euro (50 words)
- What will the Euro mean for people? (40 words)
- The European Central Bank (40 words)
- Public Opinion in Britain about the Euro (draw a bar graph of survey results)
- Arguments For and Against Joining the Euro (3 points for, and 3 points against)

1 What is the main aim of EU regional policy?
2 In what way do the richer members benefit from the regional policy?
3 Make your own brief notes on:
   a) European Social Fund
   b) European Regional Development Fund
   c) European Agricultural Guidance and Guarantee Fund
4 Study the list of Objectives. After discussion in class, make notes on which Objectives you think might apply to your local area.

REGIONAL DEVELOPMENT POLICIES

Living standards, unemployment rates and patterns of industry vary greatly across the member states of the European Union. Some parts of Europe have been prosperous and successful for many years; other parts lag behind. One of the aims of the EU is to 'equalise' living standards across the whole of the community. To do this a series of regional policies have been introduced.

The Community's Regional Policy accounts for about one-third of the total budget. This is because the member states think it is important to improve living standards in the poorer areas. Even the richer members will benefit – if living standards are higher across Europe then more people will have the money to buy goods and services which may well be produced in the wealthiest parts of Europe.

The Community has four different Structural Funds which it uses to reduce regional imbalances. These are shown below.

European Social Fund

This concentrates on training for young people and the unemployed.

European Regional Development Fund

Aims to assist particularly disadvantaged regions by encouraging businesses to set up there. Through the ERDF improvements can be made to the infrastructure – new roads built, industrial estates planned and so on.

European Agricultural Guidance and Guarantee Fund

Provides finance for farmers.

Financial Instrument for Fisheries Guidance

Helps coastal areas where fishing has gone into decline. To target the Structural Funds successfully, a number of Objectives or Funding Criteria have been established:

- Objective 1 – Assist areas where average GDP is 75% or less than the average for the whole Community
- Objective 2 – Help areas affected by the long-term decline of traditional industries
- Objective 3 – Combat long-term unemployment, with particular emphasis on job opportunities for young people
- Objective 4 – Re-training for people in areas affected by industrial change
- Objective 5(a) – Helps agricultural and fishing industries to modernise
- Objective 5(b) – Bring a wider range of industries to rural areas
- Objective 6 – Help areas of Sweden and Finland where the climate is a barrier to industry and employment

As traditional industries have closed, unemployment has soared in some areas of the UK

EU aid for deprived areas

Four parts of Britain are now judged to be among the most economically deprived in the European Union. South Yorkshire, Merseyside, West Wales and the Valleys, and Cornwall – will be able to claim EU grants of up to 40% for schemes intended to improve employment, housing and transport.

The four areas join a list of EU regions where gross domestic product is less than 75% of the European average. Regions minister Richard Caborn said the fact that, for the first time, parts of Britain were among the EU's poorest regions was 'not an accolade we want'. The list includes the northwest of the Irish Republic, the Ita-Suomi region of Finland, Burgenland in Austria, eastern Germany, southern Spain, parts of Portugal, southern Italy, and the whole of Greece.

Deputy Prime Minister John Prescott said £3.5bn would be spent over the next seven years, targeted at the neediest areas. The money is additional to £3bn under EU structural funds. About 160 regeneration schemes in England will receive more than £1bn under the plan, creating or safeguarding 118 000 jobs and providing training for 156 000 people.

Farmers receive subsidies from the EU

COMMON AGRICULTURAL POLICY

The Common Agricultural Policy (CAP) was established in 1957 to improve the living standards of farmers and guarantee the supply of farm products at reasonable prices for consumers.

The CAP was based on three main principles:

◆ Financial Solidarity – The EU was committed to jointly financing the policy.
◆ Market Unity – A single market was created with a common system of marketing and pricing and free movement of produce.
◆ Community preference – EU producers were placed more favourably than others.

The CAP operates on the principle that farmers are offered a guaranteed price for their produce if they cannot get a good price for it at market. The EU buys at an 'intervention price' which prevents the farmer from making a loss. The EU can then store the food, destroy it or release it onto the market when it wants.

Steps have been taken to try and ensure that farmers do not produce too much food. One of the most controversial policies has been the set-aside scheme. Farmers are paid to leave some of their land unplanted and barren, rather than producing crops which nobody wants. Farmers are also given quotas for the production of certain crops so that no one farmer produces too much. They have also been encouraged to diversify into the production of new crops, and to develop land for forestry activities. Grants are also available for modernising farming methods to improve efficiency.

One of the main principles of the CAP is to make sure that products produced by EU farmers are given preference over products which can be imported from the rest of the world, at cheaper prices. A Common External Tariff is applied to food products entering the EU from outside. EU farmers are given money from the European Agricultural Guidance and Guarantee Fund (EAGGF) in the form of export subsidies to help them sell their produce worldwide at a competitive price.

The biggest criticism of the CAP centres on the cost. Agriculture has traditionally absorbed between two-thirds and half of the overall budget of the EU, even though agriculture only employs around 6% of the European workforce. However, over the past ten years improvements have reduced this figure to around 49% of the total budget. The high CAP intervention prices encouraged farmers to produce quantity rather than quality, leading to the surpluses.

ACTIVITIES

1. Why have the EU provided special aid for areas such as South Yorkshire and Merseyside?
2. In what ways will the extra funding be spent?
3. What are the three main principles of the CAP?
4. What is the set-aside scheme, and what does it aim to do?
5. What is meant by the Common External Tariff?
6. Why are people concerned about the cost of the CAP?
7. 'All EU countries agree about the future of the CAP.'
   – statement by Rosalyn Thomson
   What evidence is there that Rosalyn Thomson is exaggerating?

Quotas for Scottish fishermen have been reduced by the EU

COMMON FISHERIES POLICY

The Common Fisheries policy covers a host of legal, political, economic and social factors affecting the fishing industry. Amongst the most difficult of these is how to share out fairly a resource that is impossible to quantify and moves around across international boundaries. The CFP aims to protect stocks from overfishing, guarantee fishermen their livelihoods and ensure customers have a reliable supply of fish at reasonable prices.

Each year the EU decides the total weight of fish that can be caught for each species. This is meant to preserve stocks of some fish which are in danger of being fished to extinction. This is then divided between member states into quotas. Other measures include the banning of nets with very small meshes, and the control of fishing in areas where fish stocks are under particular pressure.

Grants are provided to fishermen to create a modern and competitive fishing fleet, and to assist coastal regions that have been affected by the decline in the fishing industry. The EU also supports fish farming, or aquaculture as it is correctly known.

One of the most difficult issues for Scottish fishermen has been the size of the exclusion limits around our coasts. British fishermen have exclusive access to a 12-mile zone around the British coast, but beyond that fishermen from any EU country are free to work.

CASE STUDY

Scottish fishermen expect quota cuts
European Union ministers have come to an agreement over fishing quotas for next year, solving a row over drastic catch reductions and the valuable tuna catches. In talks that lasted into the early hours of Friday morning, ministers agreed a compromise on the European Commission's proposal, which will still involve a sharp drop in the overall EU fish catch in 1999 because of declines in stocks.

The commission originally proposed cuts of up to 40% in some catches, because of scientific evidence that some species of fish would not survive. Britain claimed 'significant success' in the talks as the Fisheries Minister came out of the talks in Brussels with £30m worth more fish for the UK fleet than was on offer from the European Commission.

The figures still mean lower catch allowances overall for the British fishing industry in 1999 because of a desperate need to conserve dwindling stocks. The quota drop in some areas off the British coast was severe – haddock and whiting limits in the North Sea and herring off the west coast of Scotland are among the worst hit. Government officials acknowledged that the drop means higher consumer prices for fish next year.

Quotas for some catches will actually increase, including English Channel plaice and North Sea sole which go up by 15%. Britain's fishermen had warned that the proposed cuts would endanger their livelihoods, but after the government managed to secure a compromise in certain areas they are now saying that some prices will rise but jobs will not be hit as severely as feared. Overall, the total allowable catch (TAC) for cod in EU waters was set at 334 200 tonnes against 367 000 tonnes in 1998. For haddock, the EU TAC fell about 20% to 135 000 tonnes from 168 000 tonnes.

The problem of tuna allocations proved to be the main stumbling block to a final deal. This highly valuable fish, mainly sold at high prices for sushi in Japan, can be very lucrative for Atlantic fleets operating from France, Spain, Italy, Greece and Portugal. A deal was finally done without the support of Italy and Greece, which both lost quota allocations because of overfishing in the past.

ACTIVITIES

1 What does the Common Fisheries Policy aim to do?

2 How are quotas worked out?

3 Why are nets with small meshes banned?

4 Why do some fishermen qualify for grants?

5 How big is the zone reserved exclusively for UK fishermen?

6 *'The agreement reached in 1999 was mixed news for British fishermen. There were some reasons to be happy, and other reasons to be worried.'*
– view of Neil West
Give evidence to support the view of Neil West.

EXPANSION OF THE EU

Political changes in Central and Eastern Europe have opened the way for expansion of the European Union. The end of Communism, and the fall of the Iron Curtain, mean that those countries formerly under Soviet domination are now free to pursue their own economic policies. They see an opportunity to make links with Western Europe, and inevitably this would mean joining the European Union.

At a meeting in Vienna in December 1998, formal negotiations were started with six countries – the Czech Republic, Estonia, Hungary, Poland and Slovenia from the former Communist-bloc, and Cyprus.

It will not be easy to integrate these countries into the European Union. Their economies lag far behind those of Western Europe following forty years of a centralised command economy system. Income levels and standards of living are also well below the European average. However, the European Union sees these countries as a potential market for its goods and services. The total population of the European Union would reach almost 500 million people if all the applicant countries were accepted.

There would be huge costs for existing members. Their share of Regional Funds would be cut to pay for programmes in the new members. The Common Agricultural Policy would need further reform to cope with the integration of the farming types common in the applicant countries.

To prepare for the expansion of the EU – which is seen as inevitable, rather than possible – the Commission have started work on Agenda 2000. The main features of this are:

Pre-accession instruments

(i.e. things that can be done to prepare the new countries for membership)
- participation in EU programmes
- harmonisation of laws, to bring them into line with the EU

Financial instruments

(i.e. special aid packages to help countries prepare for EU membership)
- PHARE Programme – investment in the administration and industry of countries that want to join the EU
- SAPARD – a programme to provide help for farming in countries that want to join the EU
- ISPA – investment in the infrastructure of countries wanting to join the EU (e.g. roads, telecommunications)

In 1999 it was agreed to open membership talks with Malta. The EU Commissioner responsible for enlargement said that Malta should join the six countries already on a fast-track route to EU membership.

ACTIVITIES

1 Why do some existing members of the EU not want to see enlargement?
2 What is being done to prepare countries for EU membership?

4 CONFLICT AND CO-OPERATION IN EUROPE

In this chapter you will learn about:
- the end of the Cold War
- the break-up of the USSR
- recent problems in Russia
- the break-up of Yugoslavia
- German re-unification

THE END OF THE COLD WAR

At the end of World War Two, Europe was divided into two. The areas that had been liberated from German control by the American and British forces became known as 'Western Europe', and the areas that had been liberated by Soviet forces became known as 'Eastern Europe'.

The Soviet Union imposed its own political and economic system on the countries of Eastern Europe. Their system was known as Communism. Western Europe was under the economic and political influence of Britain and the USA, and their Capitalist economic system. The two systems are at odds with each other. Both sides were convinced that their own way of organising the economy and society was the best way. They competed with each other to try to show that their system was best. This was known as the Cold War.

Europe became physically divided by the Iron Curtain. First described by Churchill in 1946, it extended from Stettin on the Baltic to Trieste on the Adriatic. By the 1960s the border was fortified along its entire length, with watchtowers, machine gun posts and minefields. The Iron Curtain was built by the Soviet Union and its satellite states in Eastern Europe. They said it was there to stop the corrupting influences of capitalism from 'poisoning' their people. In reality the Iron Curtain was a prison wall designed to keep the people from Eastern Europe from moving to the West.

The UK and the USA were instrumental in forming the North Atlantic Treaty Organisation (NATO), a military alliance that linked the forces of Western Europe and North America. On the other side of the Iron Curtain the Soviet Union and its satellite states formed the Warsaw Pact – a military organisation linking their forces.

Capitalism was shown to be a more effective economic system than the form of Communism witnessed in Eastern Europe. Although there were casualties under a capitalist system, wage levels were better and living standards were higher in Western Europe. The people had more freedom – in Eastern Europe the governments banned all political opposition and spied on their own citizens through organisations like the *Stasi* in East Germany and the

The Prague Spring

ACTIVITIES

1 Describe the division of Europe at the end of World War Two.

2 What were the names of the two competing ideologies in Europe?

3 What was the Cold War?

4 Compare the two viewpoints about the purpose of the Iron Curtain. Which do you think was correct?

5 What were NATO and the Warsaw Pact?

6 'Capitalism was more successful than Communism.' What evidence is there to support this view?

7 Why did the people of Eastern Europe put up with the Communist system?

8 What happened during 'The Prague Spring', and how did it end?

9 Who started the massive changes in Eastern Europe and the USSR?

10 Why were changes necessary to the economic and political system of the USSR?

11 How did the Communist governments of Eastern Europe react to the changes in the USSR?

12 Why was November 1989 such a symbolic moment in the Cold War?

Securitate in Romania. Basic human rights were violated on a daily basis in Eastern Europe.

Why then did the Eastern European countries put up with a system that was imposed from Moscow? The governments of each country controlled the media and restricted the flow of information to their people. Many people simply did not realise how bad things were compared to Western Europe. The governments in capitals like East Berlin, Warsaw, Bucharest and Budapest enjoyed enormous privileges for themselves. Communism may have preached a doctrine of equality, but the leaders of the Eastern European regimes always reserved the best for themselves.

When there was any sign that opposition to the system might surface, or that they might break away from Soviet control, Moscow was prepared to take decisive action. This was known as the Brezhnev Doctrine, named after the elderly Soviet leader of the 1960s. Czechoslovakia was more openly defiant to Moscow than other countries in the Soviet Union. Under the leadership of Alexander Dubcek in the 1960s, Czechoslovakia moved away from following the Soviet line and made stronger links with the West. Dubcek's government received warnings from Moscow about what might happen, and when they were ignored the Soviets and their allies in Eastern Europe invaded Czechoslovakia. What was known as 'The Prague Spring' was crushed.

It was a similar story in Poland in the early 1980s. Tired of Communist repression and poor living standards, shipyard workers in the Baltic port of Gdansk formed a free Trade Union called Solidarity. The movement spread and demonstrations were held all over the country. This time the Soviet Union did not need to send in its tanks – they got the Polish Army to do it for them. The civilian government was dismissed and General Jaruzelski took over, imposing martial law and imprisoning the leaders of the Solidarity movement.

The massive changes that affected Europe in the late 1980s had their origins in the rise to power of Mikhail Gorbachev in the Soviet Union. When he became General Secretary of the Communist Party he was the first of a younger generation of leaders who wanted change. Gorbachev realised that fighting the Cold War and maintaining a huge military presence in Eastern Europe was crippling the economy. He wanted to make major economic changes aimed at improving living standards – these were known as Perestroika. Gorbachev also wanted to make government more open and accountable and to end the worst aspects of repression which had happened in the past – this policy was called Glasnost.

To finance the improvements that he wanted for the Soviet Union, Gorbachev started the process of ending the Cold War. Agreements with the USA reduced the numbers of nuclear weapons and ended the Arms Race. When demands for change spread to the Eastern European satellite states, Gorbachev made it clear that the USSR would now allow them to follow their own policies.

Mikhail Gorbachev

The dismantling of the Berlin Wall marked the end of the Cold War

This confused the Communist leaders of the Eastern European countries, who were desperate to cling on to power. However, when the ordinary people realised that their governments could no longer rely on military support from Moscow, things began to change rapidly. 'People power' led to the collapse of the Communist regime in Hungary, and then in East Germany and Czechoslovakia. Democracy returned to Poland and Bulgaria. Only in Romania was there serious violence as the people took to the streets in protest against the regime of Nicolae Ceausescu, the most brutal and dictatorial of all the Communist leaders.

The biggest symbolic moment came in November 1989. The Berlin Wall had divided Berlin since the early 1960s. Hundreds of people had died trying to escape from East Berlin to the West. Families had been split and a whole generation had grown up unable to visit the other half of their city. On a cold night the border gates were thrown open by the East German border guards and within days the wall had been largely dismantled.

The Cold War was over and the ideological divide that had split Europe no longer mattered. Within months Communism came to an end in the Soviet Union as well, and the country itself started to break-up into smaller units. The Iron Curtain, which had underpinned European politics and military strategies since 1945, was swept away, leaving a new set of problems and issues to be dealt with.

THE BREAK-UP OF THE USSR

Until 1991 the Union of Soviet Socialist Republics (USSR) was the second-most powerful country in the world after the United States. The Communists had come to power in 1917 following a revolution, and no other political parties were allowed.

Map of the former USSR

From 1917 until the early 1980s the USSR had a succession of leaders who all clung to hard-line Communism. By the early 1980s the leaders – Andropov and Chernenko – were old men in their 80s before they came to power.

Gorbachev's reforms, based on Glasnost and Perestroika, aimed to improve living standards in the USSR. Unfortunately for him they did not have the desired effect. The Soviet people were desperate for change, but Gorbachev's reforms failed to improve things quickly enough. Encouraged by the fall of Communism in Eastern Europe, the Baltic Republics of Latvia, Lithuania and Estonia broke away from the USSR. They initially declared that the supremacy of the Communist Party was illegal, paving the way for full independence in 1991.

In August 1991 there was a military coup against Gorbachev. Army leaders felt that his policies were disastrous for the Soviet Union, and wanted to return to a hard-line form of Communism. Opposition to the coup was strongest in Moscow, where Boris Yeltsin came to the fore. He was the President of Russia, one of the Republics which made up the Soviet Union. Yeltsin was happy to see the end of the Soviet Union – it allowed him as leader of Russia to become the most powerful person in the former USSR. The formal end of the USSR came in December 1991 when the Belovezh Treaty was signed, dissolving the Soviet Union.

The vast empire which had extended from the border with Poland in the west to the Pacific Ocean in the east ceased to exist. Russia was the single most powerful and largest new country to emerge from the confusion. In European Russia, apart from the Baltic States, Belarus, Ukraine, Moldova, Georgia, Armenia and Azerbaijan also became independent republics. In Soviet Central Asia, Kazakhstan, Uzbekistan, Kirghizia, Tadjikstan and Turkmenistan all became independent republics.

RUSSIAN POLITICS IN THE LATE 1990s

Russia is one of the least stable areas of Europe. Boris Yeltsin's attempts to introduce a capitalist system since the early 1990s have made little difference to living standards for the average Russian, who remains very poor. Education, health and social services are suffering from chronic underfunding, and are no longer as good as they were under the old Communist regime. Subsidies to keep the prices of food and housing down have been removed. Inflation has escalated leaving people with savings that are worth next to nothing.

Russia quickly found itself heavily in debt to Western banks and governments. From a position as the second most powerful country in the world, the change from the USSR to Russia combined with Yeltsin's economic policies created a third-world economy.

Yeltsin struggled to maintain the confidence of the Russian

Boris Yeltsin

people. He was regarded as a hero following his opposition to the military coup in 1991, but the public's view of him changed by the late 1990s. He suffered from poor health, associated with rumours of alcoholism. In an attempt to maintain his grip on power, he regularly changed his government and appointed a succession of different Prime Ministers.

Russia's Constitution is complicated. The President has a very influential role. The powers of the President include:

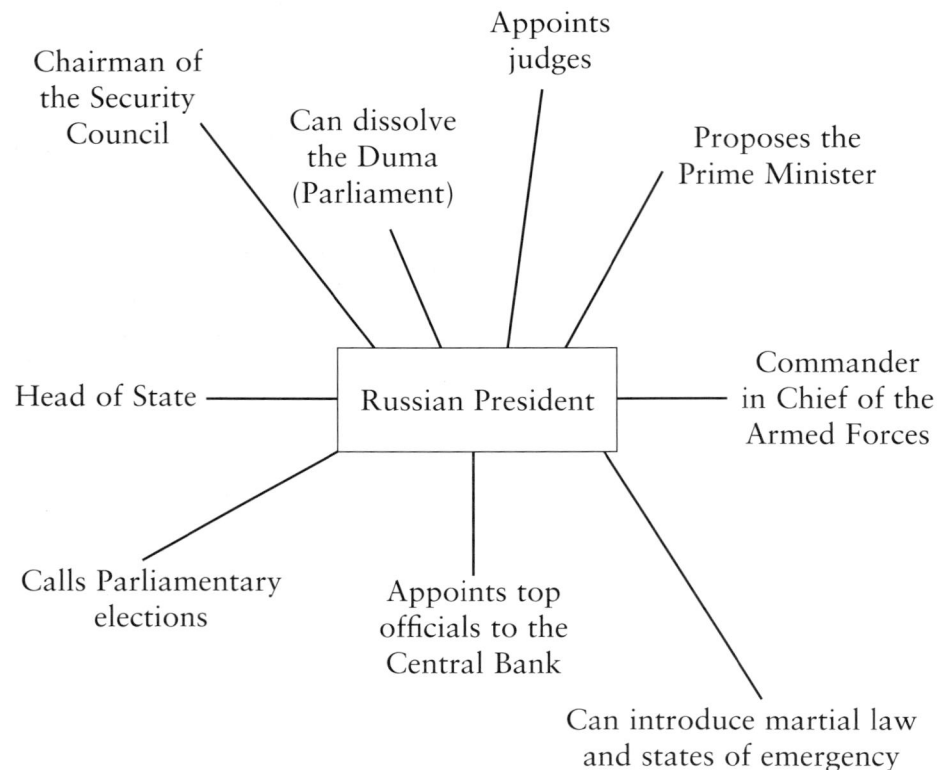

Appoints judges

Chairman of the Security Council

Can dissolve the Duma (Parliament)

Proposes the Prime Minister

Head of State — Russian President — Commander in Chief of the Armed Forces

Calls Parliamentary elections

Appoints top officials to the Central Bank

Can introduce martial law and states of emergency

The powers of the Russian President are much greater than those of the American President. If the Duma disagrees with a policy, then the President can simply ignore them or dismiss Parliament. The President proposes who the Prime Minister should be – again if the Duma do not agree, then the President can sack them. The government of Russia is made up of the Prime Minister plus the cabinet. Members of the government cannot be members of the Parliament! This means that government members have never been elected by the people.

Yeltsin's Constitution got rid of the Supreme Soviet and replaced it with the Duma. The Duma was the name given to the parliament which met before the 1917 revolution during the time of the Czars. Then the Duma had very little power and could be dissolved when the Czar felt that it was causing too much trouble.

There are two houses to the Duma. The upper house is called the Federation Council. It has 178 members (two from each of the 21 Republics, regions, districts and cities of Moscow and St

Petersburg). Each area's local parliament selects its own two representatives. The Lower House is called the State Duma. It has 450 members who are elected by the people, half by first past the post, and half by proportional representation.

The Duma can:

◆ approve the Prime Minister
◆ pass votes of no confidence in the government
◆ impeach the President for serious crimes
◆ draft laws, but these have to get the agreement of the government

If there is disagreement between Parliament and the government, the President can:

◆ ignore Parliament
◆ dissolve Parliament
◆ rule by decree (which means he can act like a dictator and pass laws himself without paying any attention to Parliament).

To impeach the President for serious crimes both Houses of Parliament would have to vote by a two-thirds majority in favour.

In April 1999 Boris Yeltsin faced impeachment by the Russian Parliament on five different counts:

◆ instigating the collapse of the Soviet Union in 1991
◆ improperly using force against MPs in 1993
◆ launching a failed war in Chechnya
◆ ruining the military power of Russia
◆ making the Russian people poorer

Many members of the Duma were also concerned about Yeltsin's frequent absence through illness and his apparent indecision.

In the event the Duma decided to postpone any vote on impeachment, fearing that it would simply create greater political chaos than already existed. Prime Minister Yevgeny Primakov was prominent amongst those arguing that the President should not have been impeached.

Less than a month later Primakov was dismissed as Prime Minister by Yeltsin, and replaced by Sergei Stepashin. The Duma had little option but to approve Yeltsin's nominee – if they did not then Yeltsin would simply have sacked all of them. However, Stepashin did seem to win favour from a wide range of deputies, including the former Communists. Yeltsin was pleased with the Duma's approval for his candidate, claiming that it demonstrated they were right behind him.

Mr Stepashin impressed the Duma with his opening speech in which he set out his main policy programme:

◆ Crack down on the 'black economy', crime and corruption
◆ Revive the military industry
◆ Ensure back wages are paid
◆ Push towards a free market economy
◆ Accept conditions for an IMF loan – Russia has agreed a $4.5 billion loan, but must meet certain economic conditions first
◆ Increase defence spending
◆ Support a Union of Russia, Belarus and Yugoslavia.

Sergei Stepashin

ACTIVITIES

1 What was the significance of the Belovezh Treaty?

2 *'Boris Yeltsin's reforms have improved life in Russia.'*
– view of Kolin Blobovich
Do you agree with Kolin Blobovich? Give evidence to back up your answer.

3 *'The President of Russia has many powers.'*
– view of Pavel Jeffrov
What evidence is there to support the view of Pavel Jeffrov?

4 Why was Boris Yeltsin facing impeachment charges in 1999?

5 What were the main policies of Prime Minister Stepashin?

Map of the Caucasus

WAR IN THE CAUCASUS

Since the break-up of the Soviet Union in 1991, the most persistent area of conflict with its borders has been the Caucasus – an area in the southern part of Russia, bordering on Turkey and Iran.

Year	Area of Conflict
1988–1994	Ngorno Karabakh
1990–1992	South Ossetia
1991–1992	Georgia
1992	North Ossetia / Ingushetia
1992–1993	Abkhazia
1994–1996	Chechnya
1999	Dagestan, Chechnya

The Caucasus area is a complex mix of different peoples. They have different linguistic and religious backgrounds. Some of the conflict is caused by disputes between neighbouring ethnic groups, and some is caused by resentment over distant rule from Moscow, Tbilisi or Baku.

The governments of Russia and to a lesser extent Georgia and Azerbaijan fear that the Caucasus could witness a domino effect. If one of the ethnic groups there achieves independence, then it would serve as encouragement for other groups to try for separation.

The conflict in Chechnya has been the most long-running dispute. The Chechens are a Muslim people, who were fiercely independent even when their land was part of the old Soviet Union. After the fall of Communism Chechnya proclaimed independence in November 1991. Moscow did not recognise the state, but at the same time allowed the likes of the Baltic Republics, Georgia, Belarus and Ukraine to become independent. In 1994 Russia sent troops to Chechnya to crush the independence movement of President

Dzokhar Dudayev. The capital city, Grozny, was reduced to ruins after a long bombardment. Russian troops moved into the city but could not keep a grip on it in the face of guerrilla tactics and terror attacks by Chechen fighters. In June 1995 Chechen rebels attacked the southern Russian city of Budyonnovsk and took 2000 civilians hostage in a hospital. In July 1995 agreement was reached for Russian withdrawal and the supposed disarming of the Chechen rebels in Grozny. By 1996 President Yeltsin admitted that the Chechen campaign was 'probably one of his mistakes'. Estimates reckoned that 100 000 people had died in the war by that time.

An uneasy truce held between Russia and Chechnya from 1996 until 1999. Within Chechnya crime and violence escalated. The government had little control over the area, and kidnapping became endemic. There were allegations that some of this was caused by the Russian secret service in a bid to undermine the rule of law in Chechnya.

In September 1999 Russian troops again attacked Chechnya. Supported by air forces, they made considerable advances against Chechen rebels. Hundreds of civilians were killed and wounded as Russian aircraft bombed towns and villages to support the advance towards Grozny. Moscow saw no need to defend their action – it was simply a case of acting against rebel forces on Russian soil. They have never recognised the breakaway government in Grozny.

It is difficult to work out why Russia chose to invade Chechnya again at this time. Many experts believe that the decision was taken by the military, with little reference to the political leaders in Moscow. Some of the military leaders want revenge for the humiliating retreat they were forced into back in 1996 when they withdrew from Chechnya.

Another reason is that in August and September of 1999 Moscow was rocked by enormous terrorist explosions. One theory was that these were caused by Muslim fundamentalists, operating from bases in Chechnya. This was used as further justification for the invasion of the area.

The third reason for the campaign may be political. A campaign against Chechnya – provided it involved few casualties on the Russian side – would be popular with the electorate. The politicians had one eye on up and coming elections, and may have believed that a decisive strike against the rebels would meet with popular approval.

Finally, military strategists in Moscow were concerned that Chechnya and its neighbouring area Dagestan were planning to set up a joint independent Islamic state, which would take over the Southern Caucasus region.

DAGESTAN

The mountainous republic of Dagestan is home to more than 30 different ethnic groups – each with their own language and culture.

It is this cultural diversity that makes Dagestan particularly vulnerable to nationalist and religious sentiments, although the local government was able to maintain stability and links to Moscow despite the war in neighbouring Chechnya.

However, in August 1999 a declaration of independence was signed by Dagestan's Islamic Council, in an echo of what happened in Chechnya in 1991. The motives behind the move were unclear. Most of the population of Dagestan seemed happy to retain their links with Moscow, and did not want their country to sink into the same sort of conflict that had affected Chechnya. Some believed that the real aim of the Islamic Council is to create an independent Muslim state embracing both Chechnya and Dagestan, in which Dagestan would be the inferior partner.

ACTIVITIES

1 Why have there been so many conflicts in the Caucasus?
2 What is the 'domino effect'?
3 Why do the Chechens want independence from Russia?
4 *'The Chechen campaign is one of my biggest mistakes.'*
   – statement by Boris Yeltsin
   What evidence is there to support Boris Yeltsin's view?
5 Give four reasons why Russia invaded Chenya in 1999?
6 *'Dagestan's people share the same ethnic background, language and culture. The people there are happy to remain part of Russia.'*
   – view of Katrina Kloska
   Why could Katrina Kloska be accused of being selective in her use of facts?

Map of the former Yugoslavia

THE BREAK-UP OF YUGOSLAVIA

Yugoslavia was one of the most stable Communist countries in Europe through the 1950s, 60s and 70s. This was surprising, considering the complicated mixture of ethnic groups, religions and nationalities that were represented. Yugoslavia was more properly known as the Yugoslav Federation, and was made up of the federal states of Slovenia, Croatia, Bosnia-Herzegovina, Macedonia, Montenegro and Serbia, as well as the autonomous regions of Vojvodina and Kosovo.

One of the main reasons why Yugoslavia 'held together' so well was its leader. President Tito was respected by all the groups within Yugoslavia, and his brand of Communism led to a certain level of prosperity that was not apparent in other Communist regimes. The state had less of a grip on people's daily lives, and even in the 1960s and 70s Yugoslavia was a popular holiday destination for Western tourists. Ethnic conflict was stamped on by the authorities, who did at least guarantee equal status for all groups.

The death of Tito in 1980 left a vacuum that was difficult to fill. There was no obvious successor to Tito who would be acceptable to all groups within the Yugoslav Federation. This allowed the different states within the Federation to vie for supremacy. Serbia was the largest and most powerful of the member states, and by the late 1980s Serbian nationalism was rising to the surface.

Serbia had two large ethnic minority groups. In the northern region of Vojvodina there were tens of thousands of ethnic Hungarians, while in the south in Kosovo there were hundreds of thousands of ethnic Albanians. These groups had enjoyed virtual self-government under Tito, but this was withdrawn after disturbances in Kosovo. These were portrayed as violence against the Serbians who lived there, and gave the government in Belgrade the opportunity to send in troops to quell the Albanians. This happened in the late 1980s and allowed Serbian politician Slobodan Milosevic to make a name for himself.

CROATIA AND SLOVENIA

Dismayed by the growing power of Serbia within the Yugoslav Federation, both Slovenia and Croatia declared independence in 1991. In the case of Slovenia the process was peaceful, because Slovenia did not have a wide range of ethnic groups within its borders. In Croatia things were different. Although Croatia was led by a Croat nationalist, Franjo Tudjman, there was a large Serb minority in the country. Tensions had existed between Croats and Serbs since the World War Two when the Croats had supported the Nazis.

The Serb minority created their own mini-state within Croatia, but the Croat army attacked them. The Yugoslav Army, dominated by Serbia, intervened on behalf of Serb minority. Croatia degenerated into civil war. The United Nations was called in to keep the peace between the two sides. The result was that most of the Serb minority was forced to flee from Croatia in the first outbreak of ethnic cleansing to affect the former Yugoslavia.

BOSNIA

In Bosnia the population consisted of a mix of Bosnian Muslims, Bosnian Croats and Bosnian Serbs. The different population groups were mixed together in the larger towns and cities, but the rural areas tended to be dominated by one group or another. In 1992 a referendum was held in Bosnia on the subject of independence. The Muslims and Croats mainly supported independence, but the Serbs were bitterly opposed. Civil war quickly broke out, with the Bosnian Serbs supported by the government in Belgrade.

Bosnia saw ethnic cleansing on a huge scale. Homes were burned and civilians were raped and murdered as a warning to others. After almost three years of fighting in Bosnia a peace plan was devised at Dayton, Ohio. Bosnia was divided into zones; two smaller areas dominated by Serbs and linked by the Posavina Corridor, and a larger area under Muslim and Croat control. This latter area became the independent state of Bosnia – the area under Serb control calls itself Republika Serbska, and although officially part of Bosnia it runs its own affairs.

Both the United Nations and NATO were involved in the Bosnian conflict. The UN's diplomatic initiatives were ineffective until they were backed by decisive military action by NATO forces.

KOSOVO

The southern Serbian province of Kosovo was always likely to be a flashpoint in the break-up of Yugoslavia. In the mid 1990s the population of the province was split between Serbians (approximately 30%) and ethnic Albanians (approximately 70%). The Serbians regarded Kosovo as an important part of Serbia because of historic battles that had been fought and won there in the past. The ethnic Albanians saw themselves as a different ethnic group, and wanted independence or unification with Albania.

The Kosovo Liberation Army (KLA) was formed as a terrorist and guerrilla group that fought a campaign against the Serbian rulers. They gained support from Albania, and indirectly from the USA and elsewhere in the form of arms and ammunition. In early 1999 the Serbian Army sent large numbers of troops to Kosovo in an attempt to quell disturbances and to deal with the terrorist activities of the KLA.

With the support of the Serbian Army, local Serbs began a process of ethnic cleansing that was to drive upwards of one million ethnic Albanians from their homes. They fled across the borders into Albania and Macedonia, with tales of horrific massacres and brutal torture.

The outside world was forced to take action. This was the biggest campaign of ethnic cleansing seen in Europe since World War Two, and further evidence of Serbian aggression led by President Slobodan Milosevic. NATO began a bombing campaign against economic and military targets in Serbia and Kosovo, aimed at forcing the Serbian Army to withdraw from Kosovo.

The air war against Serbia caused enormous damage. Major bridges and routeways were destroyed, and industrial areas devastated. NATO accepted that there would be some 'collateral damage' – their way of defining civilian casualties. When the air strikes began, the Serbs stepped up their ethnic cleansing campaign against Albanians in Kosovo, but the Albanians continued to support the actions of the USA and the UK – the two countries most directly involved. The Albanians believed that something had to be done about Milosevic, or else they would never be able to return to their homes.

After several months of bombing the ordinary Serbian people were starting to suffer. The economy had collapsed, and international trade sanctions meant shortages of basic items. Milosevic decided to negotiate, and won a compromise deal. His forces were given ten days to pull out of Kosovo, and in that time they destroyed vast areas of land and torched whole villages and towns. When the Albanian refugees returned many found nothing but rubble where they used to live.

As the Serbs pulled out, NATO forces moved in under the banner of KFOR. They supervised the return of Albanians to their homes, and were also supposed to protect the Serb civilian minority who had chosen to remain in Kosovo. In the event they were able to do little to protect them, and most of them fled to Serbia for safety, fearing reprisals from Kosovan Albanians.

ACTIVITY

Compile a time-line showing the break-up of Yugoslavia, from 1980 to 1999.

CASE STUDY

Massacres in Kosovo

Forensic experts investigated a mass grave in the south-western Kosovan town of Orahovac. They exhumed 15 sets of human remains out of an estimated total of up to 90. The head of the forensic team, indicated that the grave could date from July 1998, the height of the crackdown on ethnic Albanian rebels by Yugoslav government forces.

This would make it one of the earliest mass graves in Kosovo. The UN war crimes tribunal in The Hague said five Serbs had been arrested near Orahovac at the end of September on suspicion of murder. 'It's not easy to find out the cause of death because what we find is mostly bones,' said one of the forensic experts. The team exhibited clothing, earrings and other items found in the grave in the hope that some of the victims could be identified.

Local residents directed members of the team to the site, near the town cemetery. Forensic scientists working for the war crimes tribunal investigated more than 150 mass grave sites in Kosovo after June 1999, when Nato troops moved into the province on the heels of retreating Serb forces. They recovered thousands of bodies, but there are hundreds more possible sites that have not been examined.

Recovered bodies are identified whenever possible, and reburied in proper plots. One day in June 1999, 34 dead were reburied in ceremonies at Plocica, 60km (35 miles) southwest of Pristina, and Gornja Brnjica, 7km (four miles) south of Pristina.

CASE STUDY

Mitrovica: a divided town – September 1999

Mitrovica, a town of 60 000 people, illustrates the conflict between Serbs and Albanians in Kosovo. The Serbs control the northern side of the river Ibar, and are refusing to allow non-Serbs to cross the river. On the

The town of Mitrovica in Kosovo

other side of the bridge that now divides the city, many Kosovo Albanians – who returned from the refugee camps of Macedonia and Albania – took revenge.

They went on a spree of arson and looting – targeting Serb homes – and French troops were unable to stop it. The Serbs, no longer protected by the Yugoslav army, insisted on controlling who came into their half of town. The Serbs would not even allow Kosovo Albanians to visit the hospital, which is in their part of town. French KFOR troops had to stand by and watch.

One young Kosovo Albanian mother, who was refused access to her home in the Serbian half, cried: 'Where else can I go? They've taken everything'.

Ethnic harmony in new Kosovo was a long way away. Mitrovica, hopelessly divided, was a symbol of post-war Kosovo. Two communities, on either side of the river, live in fear of each other. The dream was to reunite them. The reality is that may never be possible.

ACTIVITIES

Imagine that you are working for the International War Crimes Commission. You have been asked to gather evidence of war crimes in Kosovo.

Using the Case Study, make a list of reasons why the War Crimes Commission should investigate events in Kosovo.

Look at the Case Study of Mitrovice, then answer the question which follows.

'*The two communities of Mitrovice hate each other. It may be impossible to re-unite them.*'
– view of Philippe Noir, KFOR officer

What evidence is there to support the view of Philippe Noir?

GERMAN RE-UNIFICATION

Germany was divided at the end of World War Two. The victorious allied powers divided the country into zones of occupation, but by 1949 two separate nations had emerged. The British, American and French zones were amalgamated into the Federal Republic of Germany (West Germany), and the Soviet zone became the German Democratic Republic (East Germany). The two zones were split on ideological grounds, and physically split by a fortified border. Berlin, which had also been divided between the four powers, was split. West Berlin, composed of the former American, British and French sectors, became an island of capitalism surrounded by the Communist east. West Berlin was surrounded by the Berlin Wall.

East Germans were effectively prisoners in their own country. Some tried ingenious methods to escape, but most failed. Many were killed in their attempts. The East German Secret Police, the Stasi, kept a close watch on the population. As many as one in five of the East German population are thought to have been informers for the Stasi, and every citizen had a file kept on them. Indiscreet comments about the government or the West could lead to promotion being blocked, jobs being lost or places in further education denied.

East Germany was slavishly obedient to the Moscow line. Therefore, the Communist leadership under the guidance of Erich Honecker found it difficult to react to the changes that swept the Soviet Union after Gorbachev took office in 1985. The East German communists did not react, but the people did. They learned of changes in Hungary, and street demonstrations began, demanding change in the GDR. More than 300 000 East Germans left the country and moved to the West, following a circuitous route through Hungary and Austria. Honecker resigned in August 1989 to be replaced by Egon Krenz.

On November 9th 1989 East Germany opened up its borders to the West, and the divisions were swept away. West German Chancellor Helmut Kohl immediately proposed a confederation between the two countries, but public opinion was in favour of re-unification. In February 1990 the East German government agreed to re-unification, and Kohl now supported the plan.

In July 1990 the currencies of East and West Germany were merged. The worthless Ost-Marks of East Germany were replaced mark-for-mark with the more valuable Deutschmarks. The union of the two states officially happened in August 1990, as the Federal Republic of Germany.

Industrial plants in the east, working with out-of-date technology and generating serious pollution, were closed down. This led to unemployment and strikes.

The new German government had a massive job to revive the economy of the eastern sector. West Germany had been the wealthiest country in Europe – now it had to spread that wealth over some of the poorest regions of the continent. In the new German states of Saxony and Thuringia some towns and cities were crippled by the closure of key industries. The steel-making town of Riesa was an example – totally dependent on a steel works that was using technology 30 years out-of-date, and losing money fast.

Germany has been relatively successful in rebuilding the infrastructure of East Germany. In 1990 the condition of the roads was dreadful, the telephone system was archaic and public electricity and water supplies were unreliable. By 2000 the east and west were virtually indistinguishable.

One thing that it has been impossible to change is the health of people in the east. Those who lived through the Communist era have a lower life expectancy and greater health problems than people in the west. Poor diet and exposure to high levels of pollution may have much to do this. In the 1990s it was often possible to recognise 'Ossis' due to their complexion, bad teeth and pot bellies.

Reunification has led to problems. In the east there is now a big gap between rich and poor. Those East Germans who have been included in the 'economic miracle' have similar living standards to people from the west. They drive their Volkswagens and their Audis, they shop in Karstadt and Kaufhalle and they travel abroad on holiday. But those who have been marginalised and are left unemployed have a low standard of living, despite generous benefits paid out by the government.

This division of society has led to growing support for extreme political groups. Racism has become a problem in the east, with foreign workers targeted for abuse and violence. East Germany

ACTIVITIES

1 In what ways were the East Germans treated like prisoners in their own country?

2 Why were the following dates significant in the history of Germany?
a) 1949 b) 1985 c) 1989 d) 1990 e) 1999

3 'The town of Riesa was typical of East Germany.' What problems did East Germany face?

4 What problems does the united Germany face?

5 Why have the PDS done well in elections in the former East Germany?

6 'Germany is the most powerful country in Europe'. What evidence is there to support this statement?

'imported' workers from other Communist countries such as Vietnam, Ethiopia and Cuba, and there have been attacks on these groups. Some neo-Nazi parties are banned by the German constitution, but other groups can still operate within the law. In September 1999 a far-right party won seats in the regional parliament for Brandenburg, the area around Berlin. The German People's Party, another right-wing group, held seats in Sachsen-Anhalt and Thuringia.

Support has also grown for the former Communist Party, the Party of Democratic Socialism (PDS). In 1999 they did very well in regional elections in the former East Germany. Some people hanker for the 'safe' days of the Communist regime, when life was comparatively straightforward. Individual initiative may have been discouraged, but the state provided all the basic needs for people – a job, education, health care and so on.

In September 1999 the symbolic re-unification of Germany was completed when the Parliament moved back to Berlin. The West German Parliament had met in Bonn since 1949, and the return to Berlin was criticised by many. They felt it represented a dark side of Germany's past which they did not want to see repeated.

Germany, with 80 million people, is without doubt the most powerful country in Europe. It's population, economic strength and strategic location spanning Western and Central Europe mean that Germany will dominate the European political and economic scene in the 21st century.

5

INTRODUCTION TO BRAZIL

In this chapter you will learn about:
- the people of Brazil
- employment and industry in Brazil
- the regions of Brazil
- Brazil's political system
- Brazilian lifestyles

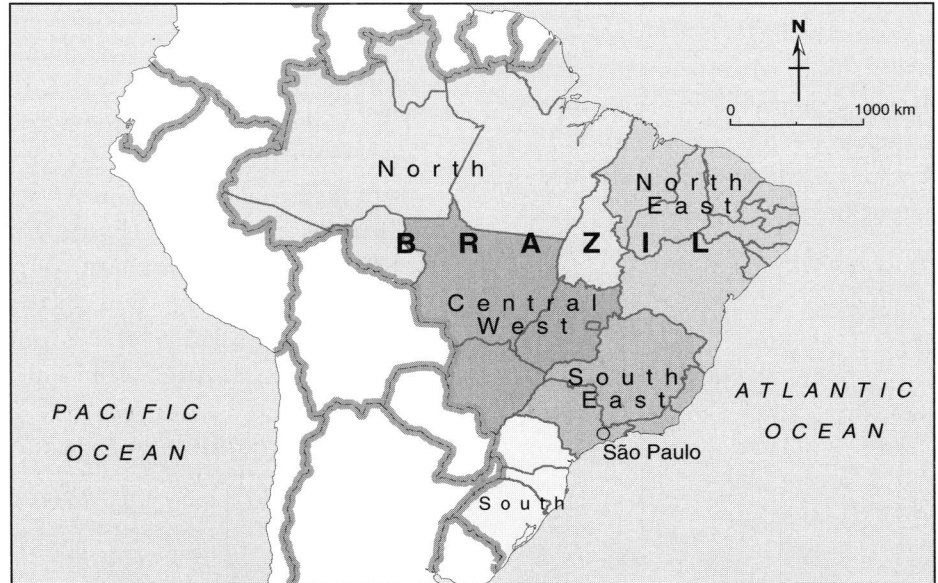

Brazil's five regions and São Paulo

INTRODUCTION TO BRAZIL

Brazil is the fifth-largest country in the world, covering an area of almost nine million square kilometres. With more than 161 million people, Brazil also has the fifth largest population in the world, and the number is increasing rapidly. It is the largest country in South America, and the most important in economic terms.

People in Britain have familiar images of Brazil. They associate Brazil with the Amazon River and the rainforest. They are aware of the destruction of the rainforest and some of the problems this has caused. They know that Brazil is a country of great contrasts – from tribal groups in the Amazon Rainforest to the bustling cities of Rio de Janeiro and Sao Paulo. The Copacabana Beach in Rio is a familiar image for many, as is the Sugar Loaf Mountain and the Carnival. The national obsession with football, culminating every four years in the World Cup, is legendary.

Brazil's tremendous contrasts run very deep. Some Brazilians have huge personal wealth, yet many are very poor. The technology and commerce associated with the business centres in the main cities is totally different to the poverty of the villages and shanty towns that surround them. The stunning natural beauty of unspoiled areas is at odds with the devastation caused by industrial development and pollution in other parts of the country. It is impossible to describe Brazil accurately without emphasising these differences, which makes the country such an interesting area to study.

ACTIVITY

Write down as many images that you can think of which you associate with Brazil. Compare these with the views of other people in the class and compile a whole-class spider-diagram about Brazil.

The Brazilian population

In 1980 Brazil's population was 119 million. By 1996 the population of Brazil was measured to be 161 million. With an annual growth rate of 1.8% the population was expected to top the 170 million mark by the year 2000. Although Brazil has a huge land area, vast tracts of this are virtually empty, and the bulk of the population is crowded into densely populated areas along the coast. The area around Sao Paulo is the most densely populated. The rate of growth of the Brazilian population peaked in the 1950s and has slowed down since then. However, the growth rate is still high and the fact that 62% of the population are under the age of 29 means that high birth rates will continue for many years to come.

Population Distribution by Region

Region	1980		1993	
	Population (millions)	Density per square kilometre	Population (millions)	Density per square kilometre
North	6.0	1.7	11.0	2.9
North East	35.5	22.9	43.9	28.3
South East	52.7	57.0	64.2	70.1
South	19.4	33.6	22.7	39.5
Central West	7.7	4.1	9.7	6.1
ALL BRAZIL	121.3	14.3	152.1	17.3

Brazil is a country in which many people are moving to the cities. People expect to find better-paid work, better housing and a higher standard of living in the cities. For many people this turns out to be true, although some migrants find that life in the cities can be little better than life elsewhere. This process of movement from the countryside to the cities is known as urbanisation. The cities also tend to have the best medical services. This means that fewer children die at an early age, and people on average live longer. The combination of migration and falling mortality rates explains why the population of Brazil's major cities has grown so quickly.

Brazilians are made up of a complicated mix of ethnic backgrounds. The native inhabitants (mainly Guarani) have been partially integrated with a variety of immigrant groups. The

The Brazilian football team demonstrates the country's ethnic diversity

City	Population 1970 (million)	Population 1995 (million)
Sao Paulo	5.9	10.1
Rio de Janeiro	4.3	5.8
Salvador	1.0	2.2
Belo Horizonte	1.2	2.1
Fortaleza	0.8	1.9
Brasilia	0.5	1.7
Curitiba	0.6	1.4
Recife	1.1	1.4
Porto Alegre	0.9	1.4
Belem	0.6	1.3

descendants of African slaves make up an important part of the population. Millions of people are also descended from European immigrants. In the case of Brazil the strongest links were with Portugal, with is why Portuguese is the main language of the country. In more recent times there has been immigration from Arab countries and from Japan, particularly in the area around Rio de Janeiro and Sao Paulo.

The native peoples of Brazil had a hunting-gathering economy and lived in the forests and along the rivers. The first Portuguese settlers arrived in the sixteenth century. Spain and Portugal had signed a deal called the Treaty of Tordesillas, which gave both countries control over particular areas of South America. At that time there were thought to be around two million native people in Brazil. It was the European settlers who used the term 'Indians' to describe the native people. Native Brazilians were used as slaves by the European settlers, and many died as a result of illnesses and infections spread by the settlers.

Today there are probably less than 200 000 native Brazilians. The Government has created areas set aside for Indians, but these areas have come under pressure from developers and colonists.

The Portuguese settlers developed huge sugar plantations around Bahia. In order to work these plantations large numbers of slaves were brought to Brazil from African countries such as Nigeria, Benin and Angola. The slave trade continued until 1888 when it became illegal. The descendants of these slaves still form an important part of the Brazilian population. Inter-marriage between racial groups produced two new population groups – the olive-skinned Mestiços are people of mixed European/Indian origin, and the darker-skinned Mulattos are of mixed European/African origin.

From 1808 foreigners were allowed to own land in Brazil. This was a major boost to immigration from Europe. In the nineteenth and twentieth centuries several million Europeans migrated to Brazil. Most came from Portugal and Italy, but there have also been migrants from Poland and Germany. Germans and Italians have set up successful farms in the south.

In the later twentieth century the most significant group of immigrants was the Japanese. They are important in the coffee, cotton and tea industries, and have become the most prosperous ethnic group in Brazil.

The 1991 census recorded that 55% of Brazil's population were of European origin, 39% of mixed race (Mulatto and Mestiços), 5% of African origin and just under 1% of Japanese origin.

FUNAI, the Government Indian Agency, has documented 174 different Indian languages and dialects in Brazil. Growing international concern over the destruction of the Amazon rainforest has also highlighted the plight of the Brazilian Indians, who are facing the loss of their lands and livelihood.

MIXING OF CULTURES

Brazil was part of the Portuguese Empire until 1822. The influence of Portugal on modern Brazil is still obvious.

◆ Portuguese is the official language of Brazil.
◆ 90% of the population are Roman Catholic.
◆ The Portuguese built the ports and coastal towns which became important Brazilian cities such as Recife, Natal and Salvador.
◆ It was the Portuguese who first developed sugar and coffee growing, and opened up gold mining.

However, although it is often ignored by urban Brazilians, native Indian culture also has a significant impact on the country. Many indigenous foods and beverages such as tapioca, manioc, potatoes, mate and guaraná have become staples for Brazilians. The Indians also gave colonists various objects and skills which are now in daily use in Brazil such as dugout canoes, thatched roofing and weaving techniques.

The influence of African culture is also very powerful, especially in the North East. The slaves imported by the Portuguese brought with them their religion, music and cuisine, all of which have become embedded in Brazilian identity. Capoeira, an African martial art developed by slaves to fight their oppressors, has become very popular again in Brazil.

THE BRAZILIAN ECONOMY – EMPLOYMENT AND INDUSTRY

Brazil's economy was originally based on two primary products – sugar and coffee. Sugar was introduced in the sixteenth century by the earliest Portuguese settlers. Coffee was originally grown further north in South America, in French Guiana. The hilly areas around Rio de Janeiro and Sao Paulo proved an ideal environment for coffee growing and the industry developed in the eighteenth century. Brazil remains to this day the world's biggest producer and exporter of both these important crops.

Other major crops grown for export in Brazil include soya, cocoa,

ACTIVITIES

1 What has happened to the population of Brazil in recent years? Give figures to support your answer.
2 'Brazil's population is evenly distributed around the country' – view of Wilson Piazza
Why can Wilson Piazza be accused of exaggeration?
3 On a blank map of Brazil, mark on the locations of the ten major cities.
4 What is urbanisation?
5 Why are so many people attracted to the cities?
6 Describe the main ethnic groups that make up the Brazilian population.
7 How many native Brazilians are there today?
8 Describe the ethnic origin of both the Mestico and the Mulatto people.
9 From which European countries did many people move to Brazil?
10 What is the purpose of FUNAI?
11 What evidence is there of Portuguese influence on modern Brazil?
12 Give evidence to show that African and native Brazilian cultures are also important in modern Brazil.

cotton, tobacco and maize. Rice, sorghum and beans are grown for the domestic market. Many different fruits and nuts are grown in Brazil, and some such as maracuja (passion fruit) are becoming more popular in Europe. Brazil produces the majority of orange juice concentrate for the world market.

Cattle ranching is important, especially in the South and North East regions. Gauchos (cowboys) herd cattle on the vast plains of the South. In the North East region cowboys are known as bombachas.

Despite the long coastline, Brazil does not have an important fishing industry. The fishing that is carried out is mainly on a small local scale, with produce being sold in village markets.

Timber production is important. Hardwoods from the rainforests are felled and sold for export. Softwoods are used locally for the manufacture of paper.

Since the mid twentieth century the Brazilian Government has made great efforts to change from an agricultural economy to an industrial economy. Huge investment took place from the 1950s to the 1970s to create what is known as 'The Brazilian Miracle'. Brazil is now the sixth largest aircraft manufacturer in the world, the eighth largest producer of steel and the ninth largest manufacturer of motor cars.

In the 1970s Brazil borrowed vast sums of money from international banks to promote industry. This has left the country with huge debts which now represent a big economic problem. Brazil has the largest foreign debt of any country in the world – $179 billion in 1997.

Gross Domestic Product (GDP) is a measure of the size of the economy of a country. It is a figure that puts a total value on everything that is produced in a country in a year. In a world league table of GDP Brazil comes in the top ten, making it one of the wealthiest countries in the world. However, it is important to see how this wealth is divided out amongst the people. Brazil has a huge population, and when figures for GDP per capita (per person) are examined, Brazil does not fare so well.

As part of 'The Brazilian Miracle' state-run companies were established for major industries such as oil, steel, communications and electricity. Petrobrás was created in 1953 to develop Brazil's oil reserves. Foreign companies were also encouraged to move to Brazil. Products such as televisions, fridges, washing machines and cars are now manufactured on a large-scale in Brazil, both for the domestic market and for export. Brazil also has a growing high-tech electronics and computer industry.

The motor vehicle industry developed from Brazil's successful steel industry. Brazil produced around 1.5 million vehicles per year in the 1990s. Many were exported to countries such as Argentina, Paraguay and Uruguay. The aircraft industry specialises in small aircraft which are used for training purposes by airlines and air forces all over the world, including the RAF in Britain.

Traditional industries such as textiles, clothing and food

processing have continued to be successful. These existed before 'The Brazilian Miracle' and they also produce for the domestic and export markets.

Manufacturing is mainly located in the South East region of Brazil. The iron and steel industry uses raw materials from the state of Minas Gerias. Newly developed oil and gas fields are located just offshore from Rio de Janeiro. The major ports of the area are centres for the processing of coffee beans.

Brazil possesses great natural mineral wealth. In recent times the country has started to capitalise on its natural wealth. With finance from international banks and foreign investment, the Grande Carajas iron-ore mine has been developed and a 900-km long railway link created to a newly-built port at São Luis. The steel industry was wholly state-owned until the early 1990s when it was privatised.

Brazil also exports bauxite, the raw material from which aluminium is made, and cassiterite, the main ore of tin. There are also valuable gold reserves in the North.

Hydro-electric power has been developed on a large scale in Brazil. 90% of the country's electricity is generated in this way. Hydro-electric power causes minimal pollution compared to using fossil fuels such as gas, coal or oil. It also uses a renewable resource, that is, one which will never run out. The Itiapú Dam, built jointly by Brazil and Paraguay on the Paraná River is the largest HEP scheme in the world.

In the 1970s, because of the lack of oil reserves and the high cost of importing oil, the Government sponsored a plan to use a different fuel for cars. As a result of this a new fuel – a type of alcohol made from sugar cane – was developed. By the mid 1980s 85% of Brazilian cars were powered by this type of fuel, known as 'alcool'. More recently the world price of oil has dropped, and Brazil has started to develop more oil reserves of its own, so the proportion of cars running on alcool has fallen. Brazil is now the third-largest oil-producer in Latin America and is virtually self-sufficient.

EMPLOYMENT IN BRAZIL

In the mid-1990s the Brazilian workforce was estimated at 70 million people. Of these, 23% were employed in agriculture, 40% in industry and 24% in the financial services sector.

The agricultural sector is much more important in Brazil than in developed countries such as the USA, UK or Germany. Agriculture in Brazil still tends to be labour intensive but through time the numbers of people employed will fall, although output will actually increase.

THE REGIONS OF BRAZIL

The Brazilian Government divides the country into five regions for administrative purposes.

ACTIVITIES

1 What are primary products? Give examples.
2 Why is it surprising that Brazil does not have an important fishing industry?
3 What purposes are found for hardwoods and softwoods?
4 'There is little evidence to suggest that Brazil has become a major industrial country'
   – view of Emerson Leao
   Why could Emerson Leao be accused of being selective in the use of facts?
5 How did Brazil find the money to develop its industries?
6 What problem has this left for Brazil?
7 Give examples of state-run industries.
8 Where is the main manufacturing region of Brazil?
9 Describe the economic development at Grande Carajas.
10 Why is hydroelectric power more environmentally-friendly than other ways of generating electricity?
11 What is alcool, and why did the Brazilian government encourage its development?

The North region is usually known as Amazonia. This part of Brazil lies wholly within the tropics and is mainly covered in dense rainforest. Although it makes up 40% of the land area of Brazil, the North region contains less than 2% of Brazil's people. The region contains the Carajas Mountains which are rich in minerals such as iron, manganese, copper, nickel and bauxite. The great rivers of this area provide one of the main methods of transport and communication. Ships as large as 5000 tonnes can reach Manaus, while vessels of 3000 tonnes can navigate as far as Iquitos, over the border into Peru.

The North East region is much drier. The interior or sertão as it is known in Brazil, suffers long periods of drought. The coastal plain, which is less than 100km wide in places, is quite different and is where most of the cities of this region are located. The North East was the first area to be colonised by the Portuguese, who made substantial fortunes from sugar cane plantations. The sugar cane barons preferred to put their profits into new ventures such as mining and coffee production elsewhere in the country, rather than improving the local infrastructure.

The Central West region, sometimes known as the Central Plateau, is an area of grassland. To the north it merges into the rainforest area of Amazonia. Brasilia, the capital city of the country, is located in the Central West Region.

The South region has a much cooler and more temperate climate than the rest of Brazil. The population is made up of a mixture of groups giving this area its characteristic diversity.

The South Eastern region is the heartland of Brazil. Here live around half of Brazil's people, in a region that makes up just 10% of the land area. The major cities such as Rio de Janeiro and Sao Paulo lie in this area. Most of Brazil's industry is in the South East region. The temperate climate and rich soils make it ideal for coffee production – most of Brazil's coffee comes from this region.

ACTIVITY

'*Brazil's regions are very different from each other.*'
Describe the main differences between the regions of Brazil.

BRAZIL'S POLITICAL SYSTEM

Brazil became an independent country in 1822 when it broke away from Portuguese colonial rule. Dom Pedro I was the first Emperor of the independent Brazil. His son, Dom Pedro II, shaped Brazil into a pioneering country. The first postage stamps outside Britain were used in Brazil, the country had one of the first telephone systems and the railways spread over the coastal area. He introduced many reforms including the abolition of slavery in 1888.

The growing numbers of businessmen who owned coffee and sugar plantations became the most powerful group in the country. They demanded the end of the monarchy and in 1889 the Emperor was overthrown. Brazil became a Republic headed by Marshal Deodoro da Fonseca. The links between the country and the

Catholic Church were ended. The new politicians adopted the motto 'Order and Progress' which was incorporated into the new Brazilian flag.

Since then Brazil has gone through periods of democracy and dictatorship. There has been a succession of military and civilian governments. One of the most respected Presidents was Getúlio Vargas (1930 – 1945, and 1950 – 1954) who was known as 'The Father of the Poor', because of the projects he introduced to improve living standards for all Brazilians. However, the reputation of Vargas is not so strong outside Brazil. His 'New State' was based on Italian fascism and included many of the ideas of Mussolini. Trade unions were strengthened but the positions of power were filled with people loyal to the Government. Strikes were banned, but working conditions were improved.

Vargas was elected as a constitutional President. In 1937, following a failed Communist-inspired coup by the military, he became a dictator – suspending elections, banning opposition parties and giving great power to the Secret Police.

During World War Two Brazil initially supported the Axis Powers (Germany, Italy and Japan). The USA put economic pressure on Brazil to change, and in 1942 they declared war on Germany. 25 000 Brazilian troops joined the Allied forces in Europe for the invasion of Italy in 1944.

After the war the demands for democracy meant that Vargas was forced to resign, only to return again as elected President in 1950. He was responsible for the development of state-owned industries such as Petrobrás.

Vargas committed suicide in 1954, sparking off a turbulent period in Brazilian politics. President Kubitschek, who succeeded Vargas, had a vision of Brazil as a major world power. His election slogan was 'Fifty Years in Five' and he started grandiose schemes to put Brazil on the international map. His most notable achievements were the construction of a new capital city, Brasilia, in the Central West region, and the construction of the first Amazon Highway, linking Brasilia to Belem.

The early 1960s were a confused period in Brazilian politics. The country was divided between conservatives who wanted little change and radicals who supported Communist policies over land reform and welfare. The Brazilian Government of the time actively supported Fidel Castro's Communist Government in Cuba, and the South American revolutionary Che Guevara was decorated by President Quadros.

The USA was concerned about developments in Brazil. They feared that Brazil could become a second Cuba, falling into Communist hands. This worried them because Brazil was a huge market for American goods and services. In 1964 the Americans backed a military coup to overthrow President Goulart. The wealthy and the middle classes and the armed forces supported the coup. Democracy was suspended and organisations such as Trade Unions

Fernando Henrique Cardoso was re-elected in 1998

ACTIVITIES

What was the importance of each of the following people in the political development of Brazil?

- Dom Pedro I
- Marshal Deodoro da Fonseca
- Getúlio Vargas
- President Kubitschek
- Collor de Mello
- Fernando Henrique Cardoso
  Write a report on Brazil's political development. Give evidence to show that Brazil has been democratic, and evidence to show that Brazil has been undemocratic.

Overall do you think Brazil's political history suggests a tradition of democracy?

were banned. Brazil developed its economy, with substantial help from the USA. Censorship was applied to the media and opposition was not allowed.

The leaders during the period of military dictatorship were a succession of generals. They said that their aim was that the 'Glorious Revolution should restore democracy, reduce inflation and end corruption.' In reality their 21 years of rule destroyed democratic organisations, ended freedom of the press and speech and created a huge foreign debt. During the rule of the generals over 20 000 Brazilians became political prisoners, and many suffered torture or execution. At least 150 'prisoners' disappeared. Political activists were forced into exile to avoid arrest. Urban guerrilla groups sprang up and carried out acts of terrorism and kidnapping to oppose the dictatorship.

Outwardly Brazil enjoyed political stability during the rule of the generals. This encouraged foreign investment, and the wealthy and middle classes enjoyed excellent living standards. Other Latin American countries including Chile, Uruguay and Argentina underwent military coups as they tried to follow the example of Brazil.

By the late 1970s and early 80s the generals began to lessen military control of Brazil. Strikes were tolerated and some media freedom was returned. Slowly the country began to return to democracy and in 1985 the first non-military leader for 21 years was inaugurated. The first proper democratic elections for Parliament were held in 1987 and the Party of the Brazilian Democratic Movement (PMDB) enjoyed a landslide victory. These were followed by Presidential elections in 1989 when conservative Collor de Mello defeated the Workers' Party leader Luiz Inacio da Silva. The new Constitution demanded that all literate persons between 18 and 69 must vote, and that those who are illiterate, over 70 or between 16 and 17 could vote if they wished to.

President Collor was forced to resign in 1992 in a corruption-scandal which shocked Brazil. Human rights abuses were still happening on a wide scale and the economy showed signs of strain. A new President, Fernando Henrique Cardoso, was elected in 1993. He privatised some of the state industries and introduced limited democratic reforms to improve the human rights situation. He was re-elected for a second-term in October 1998.

KEY DATES IN BRAZIL'S HISTORY

1500	Cabral lands on the east coast of Brazil and claims the land for Portugal
1549	Colonial rule established
1789	First independence movement started – the leader was later executed
1815	Brazil and Portugal become a 'joint country' – Rio de Janeiro becomes the capital of the 'United Kingdom of Portugal'

1822	Brazil declares independence from Portugal, with Dom Pedro as monarch
1888	Slavery abolished
1889	Brazil becomes a republic
1930	Military coup establishes Vargas as President
1945	Army forces Vargas to resign
1960	Brasilia replaces Rio de Janeiro as the capital, in a bid to open up the interior of Brazil
1964	Military coup forces out the democratic President Goulart. Brazil returns to dictatorship
1985	Return to civilian rule and democracy

STRUCTURE OF THE POLITICAL SYSTEM

Brazil is a multi-party democracy. The system of government is based on the 1988 Constitution. The Head of State and Head of Government is known as the President, who is elected for a four-year term by the people. In 1994 and in 1998 the successful candidate was Fernando Henrique Cardoso of the Brazilian Social Democrat Party (PSDB). The President appoints their own team of Ministers of State.

Parliament, known as the Congresso Nacional, has two chambers. The Câmara dos Deputados (Chamber of Deputies) has 513 members, elected for a four year term using a proportional representation system. The Senado Federal (Federal Senate) has 81 members, elected for an eight year term of office, with elections every four years for some of the seats. Three Senators are elected from each state.

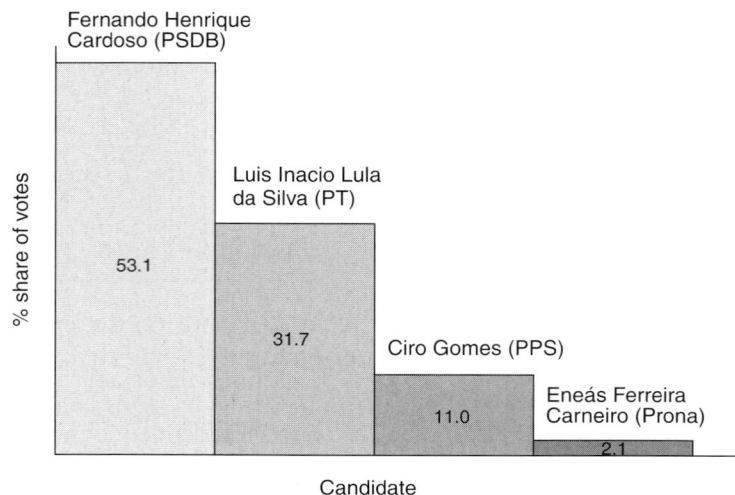

1998 Presidential Election result

State of Parties in the Chamber of Deputies and Federal Senate, October 1998

Party Name	Acronym	Seats in Chamber	Seats in Senate
Partido da Frente Liberal	PFL	106	20
Partido da Social Democracia Brasileiro	PSDB	99	16
Partido do Movimento Democratico Brasileiro	PMDB	82	27
Partido Progressista Brasileiro	PPB	60	5
Partido dos Trabalhadores	PT	58	7
Partido Trabalhista Brasileiro	PTB	31	–
Partido Democratico Trabalhista	PDT	25	2
Partido Socialista Brasileiro	PSB	19	3
Partido Liberal	PL	12	–
Partido Comunista do Brasil	PcdoB	7	–
Partido Popular Socialista	PPS	3	1
Partido Social-Democrata	PSD	3	–
Partido da Mobilizacao Nacional	PMN	2	–
Partido Socialista Cristao	PSC	2	–
Partido Verde	PV	1	–
Partido de Reedificacao da Ordem Nacional	PRONA	1	–
PSL	PSL	1	–
PST	PST	1	–

The President and Senators must be at least 35 years of age. Deputies must be at least 21 years old.

For political purposes Brazil is divided into 26 states and one Federal District (Brasilia, the capital city).

Each of the states has its own government, with a structure that mirrors the federal level of government. There are State Governors, and elected State Parliaments. Below the level of states are municipal councils which are responsible for purely local matters.

Power is divided between the Federal Government in Brasilia and the state governments around the country. Brasilia is responsible for foreign affairs, national security, economic and financial matters and nationwide policies on topics as diverse as protection of Indians and transport.

THE 1988 CONSTITUTION AND THE GOVERNMENT OF BRAZIL

The 1988 Constitutional reforms were aimed at strengthening the democratic process and reducing the powers of the presidency. Considerable powers were handed over to state and municipal

1 *'Fernando Henrique Cardoso won the 1998 Presidential Election convincingly. Nobody in Brazil can complain about the result.'*
   – view of Ademir da Guia
   Do you agree with the view of Ademir da Guia? Give reasons to support your answer.

2 Brazil has a bi-cameral system. What are the two chambers of government called?

3 *'The Partido da Frente Liberal controls both the Chamber and the Senate'*
   – view of Carlos Alberto
   Give evidence to show that Carlos Alberto is being selective in the use of facts.

4 Draw bar graphs to show that state of the political parties in both the Chamber and the Senate after the 1998 elections.

5 Why are there many 'floating voters' in Brazil?

Pele was one of the most gifted footballers of all time

governments. At the Federal level the separation of powers between the different arms of the government has made Brazil harder to run. Agreement must be reached between the different branches (President and Congress) for policies to be implemented.

Most of Brazil's political parties are still too young to have developed strong roots or coherent policies. They also find it difficult to ensure loyal support – there are many floating voters in Brazil. This can lead to politicians being virtually unaccountable – their party has no strong hold on them, nor do the electorate. This has contributed to the difficulties of corruption in government and public administration.

LEISURE IN BRAZIL

Football is the favourite sport of most Brazilians. Some club matches attract large attendances, but the greatest enthusiasm is reserved for the World Cup competition. Brazil have won this on several occasions, most recently in 1994.

An Englishman, Charles Millar, introduced the sport to Brazil. Initially football was the sport of the ruling elite, but that has long since changed. Flamengo, one of the leading teams in Rio de Janeiro, started as a club for medical students. Now they are the undisputed 'people's team' in Rio. Vasco da Gamo were once the most popular club amongst the black and mixed race community in Rio. They lost this position in the 1930s to Flamengo. Flamengo signed some of the best black players in the country at that time, and won over the support of Rio's poor – a position they have never lost since. Fluminese have the reputation as the team of the elite and these social class links are central to the core support of both clubs.

Flamengo and Fluminense have the most celebrated rivalry in Brazilian football. Fluminense supporters are proud of the fact they have won the Rio Championship more often than their rivals have, whereas Flamengo fans point out that they have won more national championships. The fixture is known locally as the Fla-Flu derby. In 1973 a crowd of 177 020 watched the two rivals play each other in the Maracana Stadium.

Club rivalries are set aside when the Brazilian national team takes the field. The squad usually reflects the ethnic diversity of Brazil – with players of black, white and mixed racial origin. Brazil won the World Cup in 1958, 1962 and in 1970. Their team featured Pele, often regarded as the greatest footballer ever. The Brazilians lifted the World Cup again in 1994, and reached the Final in 1998.

Nowadays the top Brazilian footballers earn their money abroad. Wage levels and opportunities in Brazil are restricted, so star players such as Ronaldo moved to Europe to further their careers with top Spanish, Italian or German clubs.

Other popular sports are volleyball, basketball and motor racing, with Brazil boasting an impressive line-up of great World Champions.

The greatest yearly event in Brazil is Carnival, which takes place in February or March. Thousands of people take part – dancing in the streets, wearing glittering costumes and generally celebrating.

RELIGION IN BRAZIL

The Roman Catholic Church is by far the most important in Brazil. Approximately 90% of Brazilians belong to this Church. Brazilians of African descent still follow the religions of their ancestors. The main groups are Candomblé, Macumba and Umbanda. The Government who are concerned about animal sacrifice, back magic and the use of hallucinogens have banned some of these religions. Indian people worship their own gods and spirits with music, song and dance.

ACTIVITIES

1   What is the most popular sport in Brazil?
2   In what way is football linked to the social and ethnic background of people in Brazil?
3   Why do top Brazilian footballers move abroad?
4   What is Carnival?
5   Which is the largest Church in Brazil?
6   Describe the main features of the Brazilian diet?

FOOD IN BRAZIL

The main staples of the Brazilian diet are arroz (white rice), feijao (black beans) and farofel (manioc flour). These are usually combined with meat, chicken or fish. Lunch tends to be the main meal of the day for Brazilians.

Acaraje – Peeled brown beans, mashed in salt and onions, rolled into balls and then fried in oil. They can contain different fillings such as prawns, tomato or peppers.

Canaru – a dish that was brought from Africa. Made from boiled okra, which is then mixed with onions, salt, shrimps and peppers, and fried in dende oil. Traditionally a sea fish is then added to the mixture.

Feijoada – the national dish of Brazil. A meat stew served with rice and a bowl of beans. The type of meat depends on what is available.

Moqueca – a fish stew popular in the North East region.

Pato no tucupi – Roast Duck, flavoured with garlic and cooked in a sauce made from the manioc plant and a local vegetable called jambu.

Peixe a delicia – grilled fish cooked with bananas and coconut milk.

6 SOCIAL AND ECONOMIC ISSUES IN BRAZIL

In this chapter you will learn about:
◆ inequalities in wealth in Brazil
◆ women in Brazil
◆ education in Brazil
◆ law and order in Brazil
◆ Brazil's economic problems
◆ developments in Amazonia

Brazil is home to the very poor ...

... and the very rich

INEQUALITIES IN WEALTH

Brazil displays enormous contrasts between rich and poor. The poorest people include those living in urban slums, those who have recently moved from the countryside to the cities, and those who cannot find jobs. They live in conditions that outsiders would associate with the Third World. At the other end of the scale Brazil has business and professional people earning huge incomes and enjoying luxury lifestyles. These two extremes exist within a few miles of each other.

The richest 19% of Brazilians control 54% of the nation's wealth. The poorest 10% have just 0.6% and the gap is widening. 40 million people are malnourished, 25 million live in favelas (shanty towns) and 12 million children are abandoned. Sixty million people live in squalor, without proper sanitation, clean water or decent housing.

One of the consequences of poverty is that young children are forced onto the streets to try and earn extra income for their families. They may become involved in crime, drug abuse and violence. The issue of the 'street children' is dealt with later in this section of the book.

In many ways Brazil is an advanced industrial society, with top quality engineers, scientists and managers. The business sector in Brazil is like any advanced country. Electronic commerce using the Internet and e-mail is widespread. The old saying, 'the whiter you are the richer you are' is still partly true in Brazil. The poor are overwhelmingly black or mulatto. The rich are largely white or mestizo. However, race is less of an issue than in countries such as the United States. Brazilians are proud of their mixed-race origins, and tend to ignore the fact that wealth goes hand in hand with ethnic origin.

The wealthy tend to live in closely guarded areas, and ride around in chauffeur-driven cars, often with armed bodyguards to protect them from robbery or kidnapping. This elite lives in a totally different world from the ordinary Brazilians – enjoying the privileges that only wealth can bring. Brazil is unlike many developing nations – it has a large First World society living alongside, but out of touch with, the Third World majority.

ACTIVITIES

1 *'Brazil shows extremes of living standards.'* Give evidence to support this statement.
2 What are the consequences of poverty for some children?
3 In what way is wealth in Brazil related to ethnic origin?

WOMEN IN BRAZIL

The 1988 Constitution introduced equal rights for women in Brazil. However, although discrimination is now illegal, women remain in a disadvantaged position. The concept of machismo is still enshrined in Brazilian law. Betrayed husbands use 'honour' as a defence for murdering their wives.

Twenty percent of households in Brazil are headed by women. More women are employed in Brazil than in any other Latin American country. Women are very well represented throughout professional jobs such as doctors, lawyers and teachers. Even in engineering, traditionally a male-dominated profession, one in five graduates are now female. Despite the improved position of women in well-paid jobs, the average wage for women remains much lower than that for men. Women on average are paid just over half that of men – a reflection of the low status jobs that women have, and the part-time work which they take.

Women are under-represented in politics. At national level there are only a handful of women ministers, senators and national deputies. At local level, 171 of Brazil's 5000 towns and cities had a female mayor in 1977. Between 1988 and 1992, Sao Paulo, the largest city in Brazil, had Luiza Erundina de Souza as mayor, representing the Workers Party (PT). Brazil's first-ever female state governor, the Liberal Front's (PFL) Roseana Sarney, was elected for Maranhão in 1994. Two of the five women who are currently senators overcame adversity to reach that level of politics. Benedita da Silva was a black favela-dweller from Rio and has been an inspiration to many other black women in Brazil. Marina da Silva is the daughter of a rubber-tapper from a remote rural area and only learned to read and write when she was in her mid-teens. She later went to university and entered politics.

The conservative influence of the Catholic Church is important in Brazil. This has an effect on women's issues such as contraception and abortion, which are seldom debated in the media. Despite this, and although the Government have not promoted contraception, the last fifty years has witnessed a dramatic fall in the population growth rate. In 1940 the average woman of child-bearing age typically had more than six children – now that figure has been reduced to three. Using sterilisation, illegal abortion and the contraceptive pill sold over the counter without prescription, Brazilian women have brought about this change.

In 1985 Brazil developed the idea of Women's Police Stations, which has now been copied all over the world. The first Women's Police Station opened in Sao Paulo, and there are now more than 150 across the country. These offices are staffed by women police officers who are trained to deal with cases involving other women. In Brazil they have dealt with tens of thousands of cases of violence against women, much of it committed within the family by fathers, uncles, brothers and husbands.

ACTIVITIES

1 Give evidence to show that women in Brazil have made progress in recent years.
2 Give evidence to show that women in Brazil are still disadvantaged compared to men.
3 *'Women are under-represented in politics.'* What evidence is there to back up this statement?
4 What effect does the Catholic church have on women's issues in Brazil?
5 Why does Brazil have Women's Police Stations?

ACTIVITIES

1 What are the main problems of Sao Paulo?
2 Why have favelas grown up around Sao Paulo?
3 Imagine you are a newspaper reporter who has been sent to write a feature about conditions in the favelas. Write an article of 200–300 words describing conditions there. Make up interviews with people who describe the conditions that they live in.

CASE STUDY

Inequalities in housing – Case Study of Sao Paulo

Sao Paulo is the largest city in Brazil, and indeed the whole of South America. In the 1980s the population of the city was expanding by around half a million every year. The city is around twice the size of London, both in population and in area.

The main industrial areas of Sao Paulo are located next to large working-class housing areas. Public transport is poorly developed, and poorer workers cannot afford a car. This means that they have to live close to their workplace. The close proximity of industry and housing has led to problems of pollution and ill-health.

Near the city centre there are large areas of high-rise blocks providing homes for the wealthy who make up only 10% of the population. Around 10% of the population are classified as wealthy and live in luxury apartments. At the other end of the scale, the poor and the recent migrants, who make up 45% of the population, live in favelas. These are usually located along the main roads into the city, on wasteland around the edge of the town.

Favelas are made up of makeshift houses with very few services. Electricity and water supplies are very basic, and in many cases people tap illegally into the public supply. Sanitation is unreliable.

Here are some characteristics of favelas:
◆ They spring up in a variety of locations – along roads, river valleys, and wasteland. Many are close to rubbish dumps, where people can scavenge for useful items. This can be very unhealthy. Others are built on land that is liable to flood – that is why developers have not built on the land before.
◆ They are inhabited by the poorest people and recent migrants to the city.
◆ Very high population density, with families living in one-roomed houses.
◆ Houses are built from whatever materials may be available – corrugated iron, plywood, plastic sheeting, polythene etc.
◆ Lack of basic services such as running water, sewage systems, electricity, gas or street lighting.
◆ Diseases are easily spread. The lack of running water means that diarrhoea, typhoid and cholera are widespread.
◆ Poor communication links. Because the settlements are illegal there may be no bus or rail services to the city centre.
◆ High unemployment – some favelas, close to factories, have a higher proportion of wage earners, but due to the housing shortages and low wages they cannot afford permanent housing. In other favelas virtually nobody has paid employment.
◆ Lack of education and medical services.

ACTIVITIES

1 What rights are included in the following articles of the Constitution?
   a) Article 205
   b) Article 206
   c) Article 211
2 'Most Brazilian children attend secondary school.'
   – view of Donna dos Dondo
   Why could Donna dos Dondo be accused of exaggeration?
3 What proportion of Brazilian people are illiterate? What difficulties does this create for them?

INEQUALITIES IN EDUCATION

Brazil's 1988 Constitution protects the rights of people to education. It says:

ARTICLE 205 *'Education is a universal right which it is the duty of the State to provide and which should be promoted and encouraged by society as a whole, with a view to the fullest development of individuals, their preparation for the exercise of citizenship and their qualification for work.'*

ARTICLE 206 *'The guiding principles for education are equality of access to schools, free education in public sector establishments, recognition of the importance of teachers, democratic control by appropriate legislation and a guarantee of standards.'*

ARTICLE 211 *'The Federal Government in Brasilia shall be responsible for organising and financing the federal system of education and the system in Brazil, and shall provide financial and technical support for the development of educational systems and for priority attention to compulsory schooling. Municipalities shall give priority to basic and pre-school education.'*

All children in Brazil must attend Primary School between the ages of 7 and 14. Free education is available in state schools. Private fee-paying schools, and schools run by the Church are also available. However, estimates suggest that as many as two million Brazilian children do not attend school – simply because they have no school to go to.

Although Secondary Education is available between the ages of 15 and 18, fewer than 20% of children move on to Secondary School.

Most schools are in urban areas. They tend to have better facilities and equipment than schools in rural areas.

Almost 20% of Brazil's population are illiterate. This includes people who live in very remote areas or who belong to certain Indian tribes. Indians peoples have their own languages and understand very little Portuguese.

Thousands of teachers and students have marched through the centre of Brasilia to demand more government spending on education. The Government's hands are tied by the large debt repayments which they have to make to the International Monetary Fund, which means they have little money left to spend on services such as education.

LAW AND ORDER IN BRAZIL

CASE STUDY

Robbery on the streets of Rio
There are so many hold-ups and robberies on the streets of Rio de Janeiro, that motorists have been told that they no longer need to stop at traffic lights at night. Police say that as long as drivers reduce their speed they will not be fined for going through red lights between 10pm and 5am.

In one weekend, three people were killed and at least six injured in a series of incidents involving vehicle theft. Some people were surprised by the decision, as Brazil has strict driving laws. Tough penalties contained in the highway code include prison sentences for drunken driving, and this has led to a significant fall in the number of deaths on the road.

Car-jacking has become a serious problem in Rio de Janeiro. In one weekend a businesswoman was shot dead at a traffic light after robbers opened fire on a group of cars trying to flee from them and an off-duty policeman was seriously wounded by car-jackers in the beach neighbourhood of Copa Cabana.

Going through a red light in Brazil normally carries a fine of $100 and seven points on your driver's licence. However, many motorists in the country's major cities routinely ignore this rule at night. Now, the authorities in Rio are giving the practice their blessing. However, that is not their only piece of advice. Police say that in the overwhelming majority of cases, people shot in car-jacking incidents are those who try to escape.

Far better, they say, to hand over your car or your belongings and escape with your life.

Brazil's legal and court system has a poor reputation, and many people have little respect for the law. One reason for this lack of respect is the way that the police and courts often seem to crack down hard on minor criminals, while ignoring large-scale crime and organised violence. Public lynchings have become a feature as people take justice into their own hands.

In 1992 police massacred 111 prisoners in a Sao Paulo jail following a riot against overcrowded and insanitary conditions. Torture is used as a matter of routine when interrogating suspected criminals. Allegations of corruption against the police are widespread.

NEWSPAPER REPORTS — CRIME IN BRAZIL

Brazilian police sent into slums

The authorities in Brazil have announced that they are to deploy military police in several slum areas in Rio de Janeiro, following several days of riots.

The governor of Rio de Janeiro, Anthony Garotinho, said that the police would act swiftly to prevent any further violence, which he said had been orchestrated by drug traffickers. Protesters torched several vehicles and blocked a main road following the death of a young slum-dweller during earlier clashes with police.

Seven shot in Brazilian bar

Seven people have been killed in a shooting in the Brazilian city of Sao Paulo. Unidentified gunmen walked into a bar in a poor neighbourhood of Sao Paulo and shot indiscriminately at those present.

Police officials say the incident was probably related to drug trafficking.

Rio murder rate slashed

A new report says the number of murders in Rio de Janeiro, one of the world's most violent cities, has fallen by nearly 30% over the past five years. The report, carried out by a local think tank, gave no single reason for the reduction in violence, but said it was due partly to police action and partly to the campaigning efforts of non-governmental organisations.

Rio de Janeiro's image has taken a severe beating. For many potential foreign visitors, the idea of a stroll along Copacabana beach has been overcome by the fear of being held up at gunpoint.

This new study by a think tank linked to the Roman Catholic Church suggested that things were improving. In 1994, out of every 100,000 inhabitants of Rio, 78 met a violent death. By 1998 that figure had fallen to 50. In a way, this is a surprise. The violent drug gangs which control Rio's shanty towns are still very much alive, and the city's police force was better known for its brutality than for its efficiency.

However, analysts said that a number of factors had contributed to the fall in the number of murders. Local government invested millions of dollars in an effort to integrate the shanty towns into the urban infrastructure.

Police operations reduced the extent to which drug-related violence spilled over into middle-class areas, and local non-governmental organisations waged a campaign to persuade people not to carry firearms.

Rio continues to be a violent place. Its new, lower murder rate is still five times as high as that of New York, and meanwhile, in Brazil's biggest city, Sao Paulo, the tide of murders in poor areas is also rising.

ACTIVITIES

1 Why do many people have little respect for the forces of law and order in Brazil?

2 Why are drivers allowed to ignore red traffic lights in Rio de Janeiro?

3 What advice do the police give to people who are stopped by carjackers?

4 Study the newspaper reports about crime in Brazil. Make up a factfile, listing at least four facts about crime in Brazil that are surprising.

THE DEBT CRISIS

Brazil has the largest foreign debt of any developing country in the world – well over $100 billion. Foreign loans flooded into Brazil from the 1950s to the 1980s. Western banks were keen to offload their surplus dollars regardless of the long-term prospects for the projects they were supporting. The repayment of these loans, whether they went to the government or to private companies, was guaranteed by the Brazilian government.

The oil crisis of the 1970s, when world oil prices multiplied in the space of a few months, crippled Brazil. The military government of the time, determined to try and show that their economic policies were successful, simply said that they would take out new loans to cover the increased cost of oil imports.

Then, in 1979, the USA increased interest rates. The volume of debt owed by Brazil increased rapidly from £0.7 billion in 1973 to $64.2 billion in 1980. The Brazilian government refused to seek help because it would mean accepting an International Monetary Fund austerity package. This would have made the military government look bad, because they would have been forced to cut public spending. This would have reduced their chances of doing well in the 1982 elections.

This short-sighted policy crippled Brazil. It did not do the government candidates any good in the elections either – they were heavily defeated. Now the Brazilian government had no choice but to go cap in hand to the IMF.

Debt affects Brazil's economy in a number of ways. A substantial proportion of the wealth produced every year has to be used to make debt repayments. This means that the money cannot be used for other purposes. Brazil has an urgent need for investment in things like housing, education, transport and health services – but spending on these is restricted by the debt repayments. It is suggested by some people that a country like Brazil will never be able to pay off its debts – despite repaying billions of dollars each year, all they are really doing is paying the interest that is added to their debt – they are doing little to repay the actual debt itself.

In 1996 Brazil repaid $21.7 billion. Out of a Gross Domestic Product of close to $700 billion the payments do not represent the huge proportion of national income paid by some other countries, but it is still a major factor in government spending.

ACTIVITIES

1 Why did the Brazilian government take out foreign loans?
2 In what ways did the world oil crisis of the 1970s cripple Brazil?
3 How did the Brazilian government try to overcome the economic problems caused by the oil crisis?
4 Why did the government not accept an IMF Austerity Package in the late 1970s?
5 In what ways does debt affect the Brazilian economy?

IMF BOOST FOR BRAZIL

Brazil has agreed a $9 billion rescue package from the International Monetary Fund (IMF). The IMF says it has reached agreement with the Brazilian government on the terms of the rescue plan.

The move will boost hopes that the country can pull itself out of a recession that threatens to plunge the whole of Latin America into financial turmoil. The IMF is ready to release the cash after holding prolonged talks about the country's proposed financial reforms.

The $9 billion loan is part of a $41.5 billion rescue package designed to stop the financial disaster which looked increasingly likely when foreign investors began to move money out of the country. The Brazilian economy is already in a serious recession. However Arminio Fraga, the newly appointed head of the country's central bank, provided some glimmer of hope that better times could be on the way.

He moved to shore up Brazil's ailing currency, the Real, by raising interest rates. The move was welcomed by financial observers and the Brazilian stock market improved . The Real responded by recovering strongly. Brazil's troubles are likely to have a dramatic impact on the economies of the whole of Latin America.

Concern about Brazil's economy peaked in 1998. Mr Fraga said the current loan would help cover Brazil's balance of payments accounts after its access to foreign markets dried up.

IMF Managing Director Michel Camdessus said that he expected 'good news' from the talks on Brazil's loan. He praised the Brazilian government's efforts to 'put their house in order' by implementing budget cuts designed to reduce the overwhelming public sector deficit.

CANCELLING THE DEBT?

Pressure Groups such as Jubilee 2000 argue that the only way forward for countries like Brazil is for the rich world to cancel their debts. The amount of money involved is crippling for developing and emerging nations. The debt repayments seriously hinder social and economic progress. Yet, Jubilee 2000 argues, for wealthy countries the debt repayments are relatively small sums.

Jubilee 2000: Why cancel debt?

- **Because debt kills.** Debt repayments divert money away from basic life-saving health care in the world's poorest countries. The UN estimates that if funds were diverted back into health and education from debt repayment, the lives of seven million children worldwide could be saved within a year. That is 134 000 children a week. Jubilee 2000 says debts which kill should be cancelled.
- **Because for every pound we send in grants to developing countries, nine pounds come back in debt repayments.** The rich West is taking wealth from the poorest countries of Africa and Latin America. The only way these countries can service even part of the debt is to take on new loans to help pay off the old ones. And even then, they normally cannot afford to make repayments in full – so they go into arrears and the debt gets bigger still. Jubilee 2000 says the best way to help these countries is to stop taking their money.
- **Because whoever is to blame for the huge build-up of debt, the only people who suffer as a result are the poorest people in the world.** Some of the money got spent badly. Some was wasted. Some went into the pockets of dictators. Some went straight back to the West through corrupt lending. Some simply acted as a subsidy to Western companies. Very little of it actually helped ordinary people. But it is those ordinary people who suffer now because of the debt – people who were probably not even born when the loans were made.
- **Because history shows that the right kind of debt cancellation is good for everyone.** Germany received massive debt relief after the Second World War. The Allies realised it made sense – rebuilding a stable Germany meant peace and prosperity in Europe. It also meant Germans had enough money to buy American, British and Japanese goods. The levels of debt that were agreed as affordable for Germany are levels that today's poorest countries cannot afford.

ACTIVITIES

1 What is Jubilee 2000?
2 Why do they believe that debt should be cancelled?
3 What is the only way for poor countries to pay off their old debts?
4 What happened to most of the money borrowed by poorer countries?
5 What evidence is there to show that debt relief makes good economic sense?

The Amazon rainforest is vital for the entire planet's ecosystem

AMAZONIA AND THE BRAZILIAN INDIANS

The Amazon is a very large, fragile and complex ecosystem. It comprises one tenth of the planet's entire plant and animal species, produces one-fifth of the world's oxygen and contains one-fifth of the world's fresh water. This vital ecosystem is endangered – the rainforests are being cleared for cattle ranching and industrial sites, land is being stripped for mining and rivers are being dammed for electricity. Already jaguars, caimans, dolphins, monkeys and a host of other wildlife and plant species are threatened with extinction. In 1995 alone an area the size of Belgium was destroyed.

Before the Amazon can be developed, roads must be built. This process started in 1970 with the opening of the Transamazonia Highway. This opened up areas to settlers and exposed the native people to outsiders for the first time. Since then the World Bank, the IMF, international banks and Brazilian and multinational businesses have invested heavily in developing the Amazon area. Between 1970 and 1989 around 10% of the forest was destroyed.

CHICO MENDES

Chico Mendes, a Brazilian rubber-tapper and an opponent of rainforest development, was assassinated in 1988. He had formed a rural workers' union to oppose the development of the rainforest by incomers who were destroying the forest and taking away the livelihood of the rural workers. Mendes was a folk-hero amongst the local workers, and earned international fame for his work. Mendes adopted a policy of passive resistance – organising large groups of locals to surround areas of forest that were threatened with clearance. This annoyed the developers who were used to getting their way through corrupt officials, or by hiring armed thugs known as pistoleiros.

Chico Mendes

Mendes knew that he was a target for gunmen, and normally had bodyguards to protect him. However, on December 22nd 1988 he was shot dead outside his home. Initial police enquiries failed to find his killers, but after considerable international pressure the investigation was stepped up. Finally, in December 1990, Darly Alves da Silva received a 19-year sentence for ordering the killing, and his son Darci received an identical sentence for pulling the trigger.

The killing of Chico Mendes sparked an international reaction, with the World Bank and the IMF declaring that they would no longer fund the destruction of the rainforest.

Many other murders of people protesting against the development of the rainforest went unpunished. In February 1992 an appeal court overturned the conviction of Darly Alves da Silva and allowed him to walk free.

ACTIVITIES

1 In what ways is the Amazon region endangered?
2 What needs to happen for the Amazon Region to be fully developed?
3 Why was Chico Mendes an enemy of the developers of the Amazon forest?
4 What happened to Chico Mendes in December 1988?
5 'The killers of Chico Mendes got off lightly.' What evidence is there to support this statement?

DEVELOPMENT OF AMAZONIA

Development of the forest has continued in the 1990s. A huge new road, called the Perimetral Norte, is being planned, which will open up much of the area to the north of the Amazon river. Many politicians have been enthusiastic about new developments – Gilbertio Mestrinho, the former governor of Amazonas state, famously declared during an election campaign that he wanted 'a chain-saw for every family.'

Most biologists reckon that developing the Amazon for farming is a short-sighted policy. The soils are thin and poor, with an acidic nature and lacking in calcium, phosphorus and potassium. The natives of the forest operated a farming system known as slash and burn. They would clear a small area of forest and burn the vegetation. This created a relatively fertile ash. After a few years, when the soil was exhausted, they would move on and carry out the same process somewhere else. Modern large-scale farming techniques do not give the jungle soils the opportunity to recover.

Developers buy areas of forest for a variety of reasons. Many are more interested in the potential wealth that lies in the underground mineral resources. However, Brazilian law requires them to work at least one-third of the land. To get round this law they burn the forest, plant some grasses and raise cattle. This means that the government recognises their ownership of the land and allows them to extract any minerals they can find.

The Indian tribes of Amazonia have felt the worst effects of development. The new roads have attracted settlers and miners (garimpeiros) to their territories. Other areas of land have been lost to hydro-electric power schemes. Balbina (Amazonas State) and Tucurui (Para state) are amongst the biggest schemes (see the map on page 45). The Balbina Dam has flooded an area of over 2000 square kilometres. Over 70 major Hydro Electric Power schemes are planned for the Amazon area by 2010.

The garimpeiros prospect mainly for gold. They use a technique called mercury separation to extract gold from its ore. Large amounts of mercury, a highly poisonous substance, have been washed into the water where it becomes a major health hazard for local people, wildlife and the prospectors themselves.

ACTIVITIES

1 What was the aim of Gilbertio Mestrinho?
2 Why is the amazon forest not suitable for farming?
3 Why did the native people use slash and burn farming?
4 For what reasons do developers buy large areas of the forest?
5 Who are the garimpeiros?

Native Amazonian Indians

THE BURNING OF THE FOREST

The burning of the forest has caused worldwide outrage. Scientists agree that the torching of such a vast area of woodland has a marked effect on the world's climate patterns, and speeds up the Greenhouse Effect. The smoke given off by the fires is trapped in the Earth's upper atmosphere, creating an insulating layer that causes the atmosphere to heat-up. The heat from the Sun passes through this layer, but when it is reflected by the Earth's surface it becomes trapped in the atmosphere.

THE AMAZON INDIANS

The government Indian agency, Fundacao Nacional do India (FUNIA), states that there are 174 different Indian languages and dialects, and almost as many different customs and belief systems. At present there are thought to be around 200 000 Amazon Indians living in the forest, but the destruction of the rainforest has brought their problems to worldwide attention. Between two and three hundred different tribes have been identified, and around 40 of those discovered have had no real contact with outsiders.

FUNIA has been criticised for adopting a patronising approach towards the Indians. They have the task of protecting Indian areas, meeting their medical and educational needs, and contacting and pacifying newly-discovered tribes. The organisation is underfunded and understaffed. They have recently started using satellite images to monitor the destruction of the forest and to warn of encroachment by developers into the areas reserved for Indians.

Since the 1980s some Indian groups have taken matters into their own hands to try and protect their way of life. The Xavante Indians of Matto Grosso state began marking out the boundaries of their reservation, and sent a deputation to Brasilia to lobby the offices of FUNIA. Txucarramae Indians killed 11 agricultural workers who ventured into their reservation in the Xingu region. In 1989 the First Meeting of the Indigenous Nations of Xingu was held – like a parliament of the native Indians. Foreign environmentalists and well-known figures such as the singer Sting were also invited to attend.

THE YANOMAMI

The Yanomami are one of the newly-discovered tribes of the Amazon area. There are estimated to be 18 000 Yanomami scattered over 320 villages. Their lifestyle is based on the Yano – a large circular construction made from timber posts and palm leaf thatch, where each family has its own sector facing directly onto a central open area. Until some recent visitors gave them metal tools, all their implements were made of stone and ceramics. The Yanomami, who live in the north of Brazil, close to the border with Venezuela, are one of the last genuine stone-age groups in the world.

The diet of the Yanomami is varied. On special occasions they eat monkey – one per person for important celebrations. Otherwise tapir, wild pig and a variety of large insects make up the protein part of their diet. This is well-balanced with fruit, yams, manioc and plantains. The Yanomami move on to a new location after a few years.

The problems of the Yanomami have attracted international attention. In 1974 and 1975 new roads were built through their lands. People from several Yanomami villages mixed with construction workers and contracted and died from illnesses such as measles, influenza and sexually-transmitted diseases.

The government planned to create isolated reserves for the Yanomami, while still allowing developments in the area. The idea was to have no fewer than 19 separate Yanomami reserves. This policy was changed in the light of massive criticism, and only a few small areas have now been designated for development, with the Yanomami reservation left intact. However, many garimpeiros ignore the laws and work wherever they fancy.

The case of the Yanomami has highlighted the problems faced by indigenous groups. Their lifestyle is under threat from a variety of factors:

◆ Threat of illness spread by incomers. The Yanomami have no resistance to viruses that they have never been exposed to.
◆ Loss of land to developers. Gold miners have moved in, and other areas are under threat from the burning of the forest.
◆ Aggression from incomers – garimpeiros are often armed and hostile.

ACTIVITIES

Imagine you are a radio reporter, sent to compile a report on the problems faced by amazon Indians and the Yanomami in particular.
Write out the questions that you would use in an interview with one of the native Indians, and the answers that you would expect to get.
Remember that you would have to use an interpreter because of the language barrier.

7

HUMAN RIGHTS ISSUES IN BRAZIL

In this chapter you will learn about:
◆ street children
◆ landless workers
◆ death squads

Brazilian street children

STREET CHILDREN

There have been many films and documentaries made about Brazil's street children. In the 1980s the film *Pixote* brought home the horror of life for the youngsters who live on the streets of Brazil's major cities.

It is important to make a distinction between two groups. Children on the streets (meninos na rua) are youngsters who do have a home and family, but work on the streets. They usually return to their families each night. Children of the street (meninos da rua) have no real family ties and spend night and day on the streets.

Increasingly, children who start as children on the streets, progress to become genuine street children. The process is caused by poverty. At a very young age Brazilian children may be sent out to work on the streets, to contribute to the family income. They work as shoeshine boys, vendors of sweets, lottery tickets and newspapers. They clean the windscreens of cars that are stopped in traffic. Some beg to add to their income, or in some cases steal. Child prostitution and drug-dealing are other ways of supplementing their income. This working life on the streets can lead to children spending their whole life there. They may be frightened to go home if they have not earned enough, or they may come under the control of adults seeking to exploit them and take a proportion of their earnings.

Genuine street children are either orphans or children who have been abandoned by their parents. Some run away from home. The street is not just their workplace, it is also their home. These children are dangerously exposed to repression and exploitation by adults – including some corrupt police officers. The children will 'buy tolerance' by prostituting themselves, stealing for others, or giving them part of their income.

Many street children are taken into care. They are put in overcrowded public institutions. There have been cases of mass murder and revolt in these institutions, which are often little better than prisons. In 1974 approximately one hundred vagrant children disappeared from the streets of Sao Paulo – they were caught and murdered by the police.

ACTIVITIES

1 What is the difference between the two types of street children – meninos da rua, and meninos na rua?

2 Why do many young children become street children?

3 What is the attitude of the police and the authorities towards the street children?

More street children in Brazil

(Newspaper Report: March 1997)

The number of street children in Sao Paulo infected with the AIDS virus is growing by 30% a year, according to a doctor at a major hospital there. 'We have observed a steady increase each year', said the doctor, who treats AIDS victims at a Sao Paulo hospital.

A recent study by the University of Sao Paulo shows that 85% of street children have used drugs. It also shows that 86% are sexually active, and 66% have never used a condom. About 4500 children are homeless on the streets of Sao Paulo, South America's largest city.

STREET CHILDREN PROGRAMMES

In Brazil there are projects which aim to co-ordinate the work of different agencies working with street children. The aims of these projects are:

◆ to prevent children becoming street children in the first place
◆ to support the families of street children
◆ to improve education and employment opportunities for children from poor families
◆ to guarantee the basic human rights of the street children

Cruzado do Menor

This project began working with street children in 1986 in Nogueira, a small town 80 kilometres from Rio de Janeiro. A Community Centre has been opened – about 120 street children and children from poor families attend the centre. There are workshops where they learn skills such as pig and poultry farming, carpentry, cutting and sewing, silk screening, tanning of animal skins to make leather, tapestry and cooking. The children spend part of the day in the workshops and part in a school, which has been built in the centre and is recognised by the Ministry of Education. The centre is also planning to establish a day nursery for the community of Nogueira. This will allow mothers to go out to work while their young children are looked after – a German pharmaceutical company is sponsoring this project.

Cruzado do Menor also works with children on the streets of Rio de Janeiro. Workers from the group will approach street children and try to befriend them. They will offer them help with medical and dental care, arrange for proper identification documents, and find them a place in one of the hostels operated by Cruzado do Menor. They will then be offered training and education with the aim of eventually finding them a job. Support can be provided to help them find a home of their own, or to return to live with their family.

Pastoral do Menor

This group gives direct assistance to children living on the street, and also works in the poorest communities from where street children come.

The work of the group is divided into four parts:

◆ Prevention: to work with the children who are at risk of being abandoned or who are living in sub-human conditions.
◆ Contact: to approach children who are already living on the street.
◆ Assistance: to give street children food and shelter, and to look for the families of the children, in order to re-integrate the children into the communities in which they were brought up.
◆ Training: to teach them to read and write and give them some form of trade, so that they may work and help themselves and their families when necessary.

The Pastoral runs houses in some of the poorest areas of Rio de Janeiro. These serve as nurseries during the day, and hostels for street children at night. This is part of their strategy to prevent children ending up on the street. They also run a bus to contact street children, which has space for 16 children to sleep. The bus tours the worst areas of Rio de Janeiro at night and offers a place to children that they can find.

Family support is considered by the Pastoral to be the most important part of its strategy in helping the street children. The Pastoral tries to re-integrate the children with their families, and provides assistance such as supplying food, passing on job offers and attending to health matters including alcoholism and drug abuse. When the child returns home, the Pastoral will visit the home over a long period of time to ensure that the child is being well looked-after.

Training is organised to try and prepare street children for proper work. Basic skills are taught and children then given placements with large companies. Amongst the organisations that support the Pastoral's training initiatives are the Local Government of Rio de Janeiro, the City Press, the Foundation of Parks and Gardens, the Rio Zoo Foundation and the Local Transport Authority.

Roda Viva

Education is one of the biggest problems in Brazil. In 1988 Roda Viva was formed as a pressure group involving educators, doctors, social scientists and scientists. Its aim was to contribute technically and politically to the construction of citizenship for disadvantaged young people.

Roda Viva has three levels of action: direct action, intermediate action and political action.

Direct action involves working with children in shanty towns such as Borel in the Tijuca district of Rio de Janeiro. Children are given opportunities to learn and become an integral part of their families. The hope is that they will then be less likely to move away as street children.

Intermediate action involves collecting data and information about street children and the poorer children in the shanty towns. This information is then used to publicise the problems of street children. The aim is to win over the minds of middle-class Brazilians, and make them determined to do something about the problems faced by street children.

Political action involves Roda Viva representatives being placed on national and local committees and bodies concerned with the rights of children. Roda Viva can then put their points across to the people who make decisions and control the finances of local and national governmental programmes.

ACTIVITY

Using the information provided about street children, compile a report using the following headings:
- Why Children become Street Children
- How Street Children Survive
- Organisations that Help Street Children

Your report should be around 250–300 words in length.

LANDLESS MOVEMENT

Although around a quarter of Brazilians live in rural areas, very few of them own their own land. Landowners are very powerful people – 80% of the land in Brazil is owned by just 5% of the people. 4.8 million families live with no land at all. There has been considerable violence between people who want to start small farms and the wealthy landowners, who hire gunmen to threaten or even kill the would-be settlers. Huge areas of Brazil have been given over to cattle-ranching, but the landless labourers believe that they should have the right to farm these areas.

An official report by the World Bank, published in 1998, highlighted some of Brazil's problems:
- About 50% of Brazil's poor live in rural areas. Rural poverty is twice that of the main cities.
- The state of North East Brazil has 20% of the land area, 30% of the population, but over 60% of Brazil's poor.
- Brazil has one of the most unequal distributions of income and assets in the world.
- Brazil has one of the most unequal distributions of land ownership of the world.
- Limited access to land and extreme inequality in land ownership are central factors contributing to rural poverty in Brazil.

The Sem Terra Movement (MST) began in 1984 when, tired of official promises, a group of rural activists decided that the best way to achieve land reform in Brazil would be through direct action. The organisation claimed to represent 4.5 million landless families, who scraped a living from small-scale tenant farms. MST used the slogan 'Occupy, Resist and Produce' to publicise their campaign. The MST has the support of some of Brazil's churches, and many of the progressive Trade Unions.

MST occupied large farms and estates all over Brazil. They planned their occupations carefully – choosing areas of land which the Brazilian government would officially describe as 'unproductive'. Under Brazilian law this means that if the farmers move in and take over the land, the Government must let them stay and compensate

Protestors from the MST

the land owners for the land they have lost. The Federal Land Reform Agency (INCRA) operates this programme. Since 1984 it is believed that more than 22 million acres of land have been settled in this way, and 131 000 families have become owner-farmers. In many cases the peasant farmers had to occupy the land several times, having been thrown off by the police each time they tried to take it over. INCRA now aims to resettle 100 000 families per year, but they are a long way short of this target.

The MST provides technical assistance for the farmers, and employs 2800 teachers to work in schools established on the new settlements. The MST produce their own daily newspaper and broadcast community radio stations. They are committed to improving the status of women within settler communities – traditionally women in Brazil have been in a subservient role. In many ways the MST works in a similar way to the Palestine Liberation Organisation (PLO) in the Gaza Strip area of the Middle East. They provide a government and social organisation for a people who do not have political power.

The new farmers have found it difficult to make a success of their farms. A few have failed, abandoning their farms, but most have persevered. To make a success of their enterprise, some of the small farmers have set up co-operatives with others, to share the costs and reduce the overheads. In 1991 the United Nations Food and Agricultural Organisation (FAO) carried out a survey of the new farmers, and found that average incomes and productivity were much higher than the national average.

The MST leadership are very secretive. They fear assassination attempts by wealthy landowners, so the organisation is run by collective leadership. Some people have accused the MST of running secret training camps to teach landless labourers guerrilla tactics, to help them take over areas of land.

The authorities sometimes take a very hard line with settlers. In 1995 in Corumbiara, in the Amazon province of Rondonia, police surrounded 600 families who had occupied a ranch before dawn and ten people, including a seven-year-old child, were shot dead. Two policemen also died. In April 1996 in Eldorado do Carajas, in Para state, police fired on a group who were on a protest march to the city of Belem, killing nineteen men. In both cases the police were accused of executing people who had already been detained and were offering no resistance. The accusation was that local ranchers and landowners paid off the police to carry out these acts, and that the police later destroyed evidence in order to hamper the investigations.

THE POPULAR MARCH

In 1999 the MST organised a protest march from Rio de Janeiro to Brasilia, to draw attention to the problem of landless labourers.

ACTIVITIES

1 'Land in Brazil is evenly divided amongst the people.' Give evidence to show that this statement is exaggerated.
2 What problems were highlighted in the World Bank Report on Brazil?
3 What is the Sem Terra Movement, and what are its aims?
4 What success has the MST enjoyed?
5 Why can setting up cooperatives help small farmers to survive?
6 Why are the MST leadership so secretive?
7 What is the attitude of the authorities towards settlers?

Interview with Costas Stabilo – MST National Board Member
How far is it from Rio to Brasilia?
It is more than 1500 kilometres. The marchers walk between 25 and 35 kilometres each day.
Aren't conditions difficult for marching in Brazil?
Yes, it's very hot. The marchers get up early and start before 6am. They march until midday, then stop. They set up camp, and try to get publicity for the movement at the places they are staying.
What is the objective of the march?
We want to show the Brazilian people that they can take effective action against their government. We want people to realise that they have political power, and they can show it in other ways apart from voting. We also want to publicise the problems faced by the Brazilian economy.
So the march is about more than just landless labourers?
Yes, landless labourers are part of the problem. But we really want to change the economic system in Brazil. We need to suspend repayments of Brazil's debt – this is crippling the country. We also need to break the treaty with the International Monetary Fund, and confiscate the high profits that the banks make. A popular government could be installed and resources divided more equally to improve the wealth of ordinary people.
What you are talking about sounds like a revolution?
In a sense that is what it would be. In the medium to long term a popular project means reorganising the Brazilian economy and state to resolve the structural problems faced by our country: the concentration of wealth and income, the control of the media, the centralisation of financial capital, dependency on outside countries and the tragic colonial heritage.

The Brazilian Government has made land available in the Amazon Region, but this has been problematic. It is difficult to earn a living from small-scale farming in Amazonia, and farmers have often been forced to sell their land on to larger landowners.

CASE STUDY

Brazilian Police not guilty of murder
Three Brazilian police officers have been acquitted of the murder of landless farm workers in the Amazon region. Nineteen workers were killed when police broke up a demonstration over land reform in 1996.

The policemen were among 150 officers on trial – the largest number of defendants in a single case in Brazil's history. When the verdict was announced, the three men – Mario Colares Pantoja, Jose Maria Pereira de Oliviera and Raimundo Almendra Lameira – left court to shouts of abuse from people in the public gallery.

During the trial, a video was shown of the clash between police and

ACTIVITIES

Imagine that you are taking part in the popular march. Write a letter to a newspaper, explaining why you are taking part in the march, what you hope to achieve, and also describe the march and the people involved.

protesters. According to the prosecution, it showed an uniformed officer firing a sub-machine gun into the crowd. But the defence argued that the police were not to blame for the deaths. It said they had been caught in the middle of a larger fight between the state government and the workers.

The images, which were broadcast on Brazilian television, caused a national scandal and created a cause celebre for the landless peoples' movement. The defendants are being judged in small groups, with the officers who commanded the operation appearing in the dock first.

The fact that these three officers have been found not guilty has come as a blow to legal rights groups in Brazil who campaigned for the trial. The case against the remaining officers is expected to last until the end of the year.

ACTIVITIES

From the information provided, do you think the police officers were guilty or not? Give reasons for your answer.

ACTIVITIES

1 List some statistics about killings in Brazil that would shock people.
2 Why do the police ignore the activities of some of the death squads?

DEATH SQUADS

In 1994 Amnesty International published a report about Human Rights abuses in Brazil, entitled 'Beyond Despair'. In 1991 alone the Sao Paulo police killed 1140 civilians in the course of their duty. Another 1359 were killed in 1992. Nobody would deny that the police may cause fatalities when dealing with armed criminals, but these figures are enormous – even when compared with supposedly violent societies such as the United States.

In Rio de Janeiro the activities of death squads have come under close scrutiny. Death Squads have become established in Brazil over a period of years. The police are often involved with them, either in supporting or ignoring their activities. Corrupt politicians support the Death Squads, who carry out instant and summary justice against their opponents. Some Death Squads are criminal gangs who kill to defend their territory where they control the drug-market. Others are vigilante groups who will carry out contract killings, or kill and steal the possessions of their victims. In Rio de Janeiro some 1200 people fell victim, to the death squads each year in the mid 1990s.

8 INTRODUCTION TO CHINA

Map of China's provinces

INTRODUCTION TO CHINA

China is the most heavily populated country in the world. Just under one-quarter of the human race are Chinese – it has more than four times as many people as the USA, and twenty-five times as many as Britain. China is also the world's last great Communist power. Communism has died in the Soviet Union, leaving China alone as the last bastion of an ideology that has split the world apart.

China has changed dramatically in recent years. It is not long since it was a closed country, unknown to the West. Now, through tourism, commerce and trade, China is an emerging trading partner for both the United States and Europe. The people of China represent a vast untapped market for the world's businesses.

ACTIVITIES

Write down as many ideas or images that you can think of related to China. Put these together for the whole class to produce a spider-diagram.

CHINA PROFILE

Population	1 232 083 000 (1996)
Area	9 562 036 square km
Capital City	Beijing, 10 900 000 people (twice as many as the whole of Scotland)
Currency	Yuan renminbi
Peoples	There are 56 official recognised nationalities. Han Chinese make up 92% of the population. The next biggest groups are Chuang (1.4%), Manchu (0.9%) and Hui (0.8%)

THE REGIONS OF CHINA

China's provinces can be divided into seven main geographic areas:

Inner Mongolia and the Silk Road

This is a huge area in the north of the country, bordering on Mongolia and Russia. The native peoples, the Mongolians and the Uygurs, have been upset by a large influx of Chinese. The area is given the name 'The Silk Road' because it has been a vital trading route for many centuries, linking China with Central Asia and the West.

Xinjiang
Population 16.9 million.
Remote and desolate, with vast deserts. Location of China's nuclear test site.

Gansu
Population 24.7 million.
A rugged, barren province of mountains and deserts.

Ningxja
Population – 5.2 million.
Almost entirely agricultural. A remote and seldom-visited part of China.

Inner Mongolia
Population – 23.1 million.
Mainly grassland. Pastoral farming is the main occupation.

Sichaun and the Tibetan Plateau

Sichaun is the largest and most heavily populated region of China. It lies to the east of Tibet, a formerly independent country that has been occupied by Chinese forces since 1950. This region is home to many rare species of plants and animals, including the giant panda.

Xizand (Tibet)
Population – 2.4 million.
Mountainous and inaccessible. Annexed by China in 1950.

Qinghai
Population – 4.9 million.
The region where China has sent most of its political prisoners.

Sichuan
Population – 84.3 million.
Eastern Sichaun has one of the densest rural populations in the world – an intensively farmed area.

South West China

Bordering on Vietnam, Laos and Burma, this area contains most of China's minority population groups. The biggest minority – the Zhuang – live in Guangxi.

Yunnan
Population – 40.4 million.
Attractive tourist destination. Little industry, and poor by Chinese standards.

Guizhou
Population – 35.6 million.
Once described as 'a place of sunless sky, endless hills and penniless people'.

Guangxi
Population – 45.9 million.
One of the poorest provinces in China.

South China

This part of China has made enormous economic progress in recent years. It includes Hong Kong (returned to China in 1997) and Macau (returned in 1999).

Hunan
Population 64.3 million.
Amazing scenery attracts tourists. One of the poorer agricultural regions.

Jiangxi
Population 41.1 million.
Mixed agricultural and industrial province.

Zhejiang
Population 43.4 million.
One of the smallest provinces in China, but traditionally one of the most prosperous. Intensive farming brought much of the wealth. Also an important trading and port area.

Fujian
Population 32.6 million.
Coastal area which has seen much investment from Taiwan.

Guangdong
Population 69.6 million.
An economic powerhouse, featuring two of China's Special Economic Zones.

Hong Kong
Population 6.31 million.
Former British colony, returned to China in 1997.

Macau
Population 400 000.
Former Portuguese colony, handed back to China in 1999.

Hainan Island
Population 7.3 million.
Island off the south coast of China, popular with Chinese holidaymakers.

The Yangtze Region

The Yangtze River divides China into North and South. The valley of the Yangtze is an important routeway and an emerging commercial centre. Shanghai lies at the mouth of the Yangtze River.

Hubei
Population – 58.3 million.
Centred on Wuhan, the Yangtze River flows through this province. Important industries, rich farmland – and also the location for the Three Gorges Project.

Anhui
Population 60.1 million.
An area seldom visited by tourists. Anhui is an industrial and farming province, although it has not seen the rapid changes experienced by some other parts of China in recent years.

Shanghai
Population 14.2 million.
Shanghai was the centre of western involvement in China back in the early years of the twentieth century. It has recaptured that mood in the 1990s, and is one of the most successful business and commercial centres in the country.

The North

This is the oldest area of Chinese civilisation. The famous terracotta warriors of the city of Xian date back to about 2000BC. Beijing is situated in this region.

Beijing
Population 12.6 million.
Beijing is the capital city of China. It is the centre of government and also one of the most popular destinations for foreign tourists. Sights that must be seen include The Forbidden City, Tiananmen Square and the Great Wall. Older books may refer to Beijing by its' old name – Peking.

Tianjin
Population 9.5 million.
Like Beijing, Tianjin is an autonomous self-governing region. Tianjin is an important port and

commercial centre. Many Western businesses have offices there. Westerners often refer to Tianjin as TJ, which mystifies the Chinese!

Shaanxi
Population – 35.4 million.
Much of this province is fertile agricultural land.

Shanxi
Population 31.1 million.
A mountainous province with extensive mineral resources.

Hebei
Population 64.9 million.
An industrial and agricultural province, which is close to both Beijing and Tianjin.

Shangdong
Population 87.3 million.
One of the most prosperous areas, with a great deal of new industry and commercial development. Also has important oil reserves.

Henan
Population 91.7 million.
Has a very densely populated agricultural area. One of the most fertile areas in China.

Jiangsu
Population 71.2 million.
The most developed province for agriculture, it is known as 'the land of fish and rice'. Close to Shanghai, it has benefited from the economic explosion there.

North East China

This region borders Russia and Korea. The coldest part of China, it has freezing cold winters. The landscape is not unlike that of Norway!

Heilongjiang
Population – 37.3 million.
The name of the province means 'Black Dragon River'. This area has a sub-arctic climate. Wealthy tourists from Hong Kong and Taiwan visit for the novelty of seeing year-round snow!

Jilin
Population – 26.1 million.
Came under Japanese control in the 1930s when it was known as Manchuria. Changchun used to be the centre of the Chinese car industry – the factory has now been taken over by Volkswagen, which explains why there are so many Volkswagen's on Chinese roads!

Liaoning
Population – 41 million.
Economic growth is centred on the city of Dalian, 'the Hong Kong of the North'. Richer than the other provinces in this region.

ACTIVITIES

1 Write a short summary about each of the seven main geographic areas of China.
2 'The regions of China are very different.'
Describe the main differences between the regions of China.

THE CHINESE POPULATION

China has more people than any other country in the world. By the end of 1996, China had a population of almost 1.25 billion. China's population density (118 people per square kilometre according to the Fourth National Population Census, July 1, 1990) is relatively high. Distribution, however, is uneven: the coastal areas in the east are densely populated, with 360 people per square kilometre; the plateau areas in the west are sparsely populated, with fewer than 10 people per square kilometre.

The table below shows the composition of population in China:

Sex		Region		Age		
male	female	cities and towns	countryside	below 14	15–64	above 65
51.6%	48.4%	26.3%	73.7%	27.7%	66.7%	5.6%

POPULATION GROWTH AND FAMILY PLANNING

In 1949 there were 542.67 million people living in China. The population rose to 807 million by 1969 due to a lack of knowledge about birth control, and traditions of large families. Facing a serious problem of over-population, China has since implemented family planning programmes to control population growth. Since these programmes were initiated in the 1970s, the birth rate has declined each year. By the end of 1994 the birth rate dropped to 17.7 per thousand from 34.11 per thousand in 1969, and the natural growth rate declined to 11.21 per thousand from 26.08 per thousand. The 'One Child Policy', started in 1979, is the key point in the Chinese family planning programme.

Families are encouraged to marry and have children late in life. This means having fewer but healthier babies – one child per couple is the rule. Since 1988 the policy has been relaxed in rural areas. A couple with a shortage of labour for their farm may have a second baby, but they are expected to wait several years after the birth of the first child. In areas inhabited by minority peoples, a couple may have more children. There is surprisingly little opposition to the One Child Policy within China.

In order to encourage families to have just one child, the government offers them incentives. They are given bonuses and do not have to wait so long for a house. Medical care and education are provided free of charge.

If a family has more than one child then they can be punished with reductions in benefits and allowances. Medical care and education will not be free for the second or subsequent child.

The government keeps a tight control over childbirth. Each province has a 'quota' of births, which it must try to keep to. The authorities have been very keen to promote policies of birth control.

One consequence of the One Child Policy has been a rise in infanticide. Unwanted children may be killed by their parents. This is particularly the case with girls. Traditionally in China, male children are more highly prized than girls, so a family having a girl may 'get rid of it'. This is particularly common in rural areas. Elsewhere many children are abandoned because their parents cannot afford to look after their needs. There are now around 115 young boys for every 100 young girls, which may lead to problems in the future.

Abandoned children are placed in orphanages, where they live alongside handicapped youngsters who have been dumped by their families. A television documentary called The Dying Rooms exposed these orphanages on British television, and alleged that many children were neglected and left to die.

The rights of minority groups in China are protected. China allows them to have control over local political, economic and cultural conditions and they can make independent use of local tax revenue.

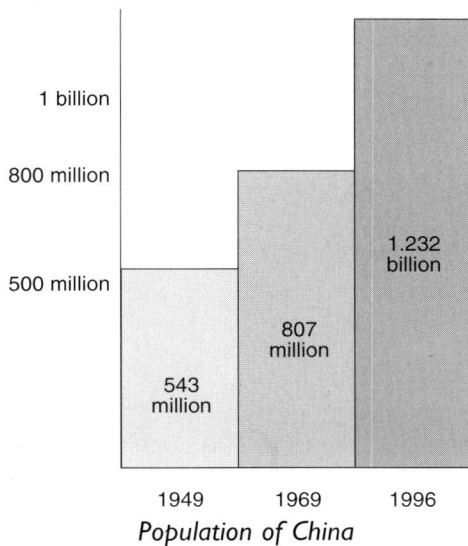

1 billion

800 million

500 million

543 million

807 million

1.232 billion

1949   1969   1996

Population of China

ACTIVITIES

1 How many people live in China?
2 'The Chinese population is concentrated mainly in the countryside. Fewer than 5% of the population are aged 65 or over. There are more men than women in China.' – statement by Chang Ha Jong Why could Chang Ha Jong be accused of exaggeration?
3 Why did the population of China grow so quickly between 1949 and 1969?
4 What is the 'One Child Policy'?
5 In your opinion, is the 'One Child Policy' a good idea?
6 What happens to families with more than one child?
7 Why are there so many abandoned children in Chinese orphanages?
8 In what ways are the rights of minority population groups protected?

SOCIAL AND ECONOMIC ISSUES IN CHINA

In this chapter you will learn about:
- ◆ housing, education and health-care in China
- ◆ differences between living standards in urban and rural areas
- ◆ agriculture and industry in China
- ◆ environmental issues in China

Overcrowding is a big problem in Chinese cities

ACTIVITIES

1 *'The government have a major role in providing housing in China'.* To what extent is this statement true?
2 Why has the government had to turn to the private sector for help with housing?
3 Why are rural houses usually bigger than urban houses?

HOUSING IN CHINA

Under Communism everyone is entitled to a house. The state has a responsibility to ensure that everyone has a house. The state is the largest landlord, renting properties to people at very low prices. However, a combination of the great increase in China's population and the migration of people from rural to urban areas means that it is now very difficult for the Chinese government to provide what they still describe as a basic right.

Overcrowding is a serious problem. Because of the shortage of houses, several families may share a communal home. Children will stay with their parents long after they have grown-up, and sometimes after they marry and have families of their own.

As the free-market economy has infiltrated China, the government has turned to the private sector to help with the housing crisis. The government themselves have sold off areas of housing – some to landlords, but mainly to the people who live in them. This is very similar to what has happened in Scotland with the sale of council houses since the early 1980s. It means that the houses which the government still owns tend to be the least desirable and most run-down.

Private builders have been allowed to develop housing for sale. The better-off Chinese, who have done well out of the economic changes, can afford to buy this better quality housing.

Whereas housing standards used to be relatively equal in Communist China, there are now great variations in the quality of housing that people live in.

In rural China, people tend to have bigger houses than in the cities. Competition for land is not so great. However, compared to the cities, many rural homes lack running water and other basic amenities.

EDUCATION IN CHINA

China is proud of the educational opportunities on offer. Not all children benefit as much as they could from education because there is pressure for them to work if their families are poor.

Pre-school education starts at the age of three. Pre-school

education is paid for by local communities or by the large employers, not directly by the government. In a sense it acts as a crèche facility so that people can leave their children while they are at work.

In 1949 only 20% of children went to primary school. By the mid 1980s this had risen to 96%. By 1996, official figures stated that 99% of children attended primary school. Primary school starts at age seven and goes on until 12 or 13. Pupils have to go to school for six days a week. In the cities school lasts all day, but in rural areas it is usually only for half a day. Chinese children are expected to do jobs around the school, such as cleaning and tidying. Primary education includes a large political element. Children are taught about Communism. Critics say that this is a form of brainwashing.

There are two types of secondary schools. Academic schools are meant for children who might go on to university or the professions. Up until the age of 15 children study a wide range of subjects. After that, they specialise for two or three years.

Technical schools have direct links to future jobs. Again pupils study a broad range of subjects up to the age of 15, and then specialise.

China's universities used to be under direct political control from the government. This is no longer the case and they are free to offer courses and undertake research in many areas that would once have been banned. Chinese students are encouraged to go abroad for part of their course to widen their experience. Because of the high demand for university places, there are opportunities to study in the evening, at weekends and so on. China would be unable to pay for the number of people who want to go to university if they were all full-time students. University education is free in China.

ACTIVITIES

1 Why do some children not benefit fully from education?
2 At what age do children start pre-school education?
3 'In 1949 less than one quarter of children went to primary school, but now all children do.'
– statement by Jing Huan
Why could Jing Huan be accused of exaggeration?
4 Describe the two types of secondary school in China.
5 How have China's universities changed in recent years?

HEALTH CARE IN CHINA

Back in the 1970s China's rural health services were excellent. At village level people were appointed as 'barefoot doctors'. They had minimal medical training, but were able to recognise and diagnose minor ailments. They passed more serious cases on to the Health Centre in the nearest town, where there would be specialised doctors and nurses. Each area also had a county hospital.

Since the development of the market economy, health services have changed. This is an area where the equality of the past has been replaced with considerable differences in health standards and services for different people. Cities now have better health services than country areas; richer people have access to better services than the poor. As other spending priorities have risen, the amount spent on health has declined.

The Chinese government still accepts that it has a responsibility to make sure that effective health services are available for everyone in the country. Some of the methods they have used to do this include:

◆ Co-operative health schemes. People contribute a small proportion of their income to the local health scheme, and in return, get services when they need them.

◆ Community building projects. Communities are encouraged to organise people to build health centres in their spare time, providing the materials and labour free of charge. In return, they will get free health care once the centre is completed.

◆ Pre-payment for health services. In some areas parents pay a fixed sum for their children's health treatment. If the child is ill, or if the treatment fails, then they will get compensation. This provides money 'up front' to pay for the health services.

ACTIVITIES

1 Who were the 'barefoot doctors'?
2 How do health services in the rural areas compare with the cities?
3 What are co-operative health schemes?

Pie charts showing the drift of people from rural to urban areas

RURAL/URBAN CONTRASTS IN CHINA

In China the distinction between urban and rural areas has always been very clear. Wealth has been concentrated in the urban areas, with poverty widespread in the countryside. Traditionally China has been a rural economy, but this is changing.

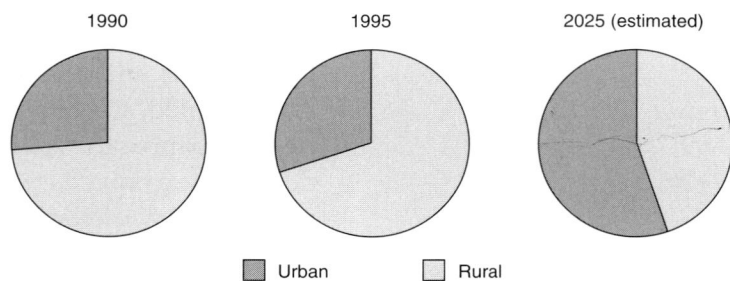

Urban   Rural

The movement from the countryside to the cities causes massive problems in China. The problems are more apparent in the cities which struggle to find houses and jobs for the migrants. In the countryside, as agriculture develops, the small farmers are not missed as the larger and more successful farmers take over their land.

Employment in China

Employed in agriculture	73% (going down)
Employed in industry	14% (constant)
Employed in the service sector	13% (growing)

The population of China's cities could double by the year 2020. Already there are large shanty towns around some Chinese cities, similar to those seen in parts of the developing world, like Brazil. The problems with shanty towns in China are the same as the problems with shanty towns all over the world – lack of proper sanitation, poor water supplies, lack of electricity, no medical and school facilities and so on. Some people can earn a living working as servants or cleaners on the 'black economy'. Others drift into petty crime or prostitution.

Many people who migrate from the countryside to the city do so without official permission. This is only granted if someone has a job to go to or is marrying a person from another area. The official identity card, or hukou, carried by every Chinese citizen, lists their place of residence. If somebody moves without permission then they are not entitled to things like free education for their children and access to medical and social services.

The development of the Contract Responsibility System made it possible for people to leave the countryside. Before they had to produce their own food – there was really no alternative. Now, because of the amount of food on the market, they can buy food in cities without having to produce it themselves.

The Chinese authorities would like to tackle the problems of the slums and shantytowns, but it is difficult when so many people are still flooding into the cities. However, if something is not done then these places could be a source of major unrest in the future.

SUMMARY OF REASONS FOR MIGRATING FROM TOWN TO CITY

Push Factors (Bad Points about the countryside)	Pull Factors (Attractive points about the cities)
Low incomes and living standards Poor Housing Lack of educational opportunities	Chance of a job in industry Better medical services Higher living standards – a poor person by city standards is often better off than an average rural-dweller

ACTIVITY

Compile a short newspaper feature, with the title 'China's Great Population Movement'.
Use facts and figures from the section above to describe and explain differences between countryside and city areas, and the reasons why people have moved from one to the other.

THE CHINESE ECONOMY

China was one of the poorest and most economically backward countries in the world when the Communists came to power in 1949. Decades of war and civil conflict had damaged the infrastructure and prevented the growth of industry. One of the goals of Mao Zedong and his revolutionaries was to turn China into a modern industrial state.

But it was not until after Mao died, and the end of the political instability caused by the Cultural Revolution, that the economy really took off. The new Chinese leadership, under Deng Xiaoping, pushed China on a course of economic reform and opened up links with the West. He brought in 'The Four Modernisations' to improve industry and farming, and started 'The Great Leap Outwards' to open up strong links with other countries.

Since 1980, the economy has been growing at a phenomenal rate – just under 10% per year. China now boasts the world's seventh largest economy – nearly the same size as the UK and Italy. Some Western economists believe that China, with its huge population, will overtake the US and Japan early in the next century to become the world's biggest economy. The economic growth that began when China accepted a market economy has lifted hundreds of millions out of poverty, and made China a major factor in world trade.

POVERTY REDUCTION

In the mid 1990s China's President Jiang Zemin made the eradication of poverty by the year 2000 his top priority. According to China's official figures, the number of people in poverty has dropped from 250 million or 30.7% of the rural population in 1978 to 42 million, or 4.6% in 1998. Jiang's goal is that 'we should all get rich together', but some of the more remote parts of China have struggled to join the economic boom.

GROWING INEQUALITY

Economic growth has largely been concentrated in the coastal areas, particularly in large urban areas like Shanghai, the Pearl River Delta near Hong Kong, and Fujian province opposite Taiwan. As a result, the poverty gap between regions in China has increased, with the interior – especially the rural areas – lagging behind. Back in the 1970s, China was a very egalitarian (equal) country – in line with Communist ideology. Now it shows some of the biggest gaps between rich and poor of any developing nation. The government does relatively little to redistribute wealth – in 1998 it announced the creation of the first unemployment insurance scheme, for example, and there is no benefit system. Now many of the 100 million state sector factory workers face layoffs and an uncertain future as the economy restructures, with a loss of status as well as income.

MAO'S ECONOMIC LEGACY

The huge state sector was part of Mao's approach to economic development. Initially, China planned to follow the Soviet model of large-scale industrialisation and the collectivisation of agriculture. Peasants were encouraged – or forced – into communes, while private land ownership was abolished. Huge investments in state factories were made, producing goods for heavy industry rather than for consumers or to meet any real demand.

Mao's vision began to change during the period of the 'Great Leap Forward,' when the alliance with the Soviet Union crumbled. In an attempt to drive through industrialisation more quickly, between 1958–61, rural communes were encouraged to produce industrial products like steel and iron to the neglect of agricultural production. The result was famine, and millions of deaths.

'To get rich is glorious'

The death of Mao and the rise to power of Deng Xiaoping in 1978 led to a change in China's economic policy. Deng emphasised the introduction of the market and the opening up of the country to foreign trade and investment. He proclaimed 'socialism with a Chinese face' in which 'to get rich is glorious.' His first reforms were known as 'The Four Modernisations'.

Peasants were allowed to produce for the market, communes were scrapped, and agricultural production shot up. Foreign factories were set up in special economic zones to produce goods for export. They were keen to relocate because of low wage levels in China. Foreign investment poured in.

China's economy faces many challenges in the new millennium. The biggest problem could be restructuring China's large state-run industries, which are inefficient and over-staffed. As millions of peasants flood into China's cities, the problems of finding employment will become severe. China's extraordinary success in attracting foreign investment may not last, and their own businesses are not well developed. China's modernisers are counting on foreign investment to help manage the next stage of the transition. Some want to open up China's service sector, including financial and telecommunications services, to foreign investment in order to join the World Trade Organisation by the end of this year. Unlike more developed countries, China's economy is still dominated by more traditional industries.

Opening up the service sector could carry political risks. China's Telecoms Ministry, for example, wants to ban all foreign investment in the Internet, which it sees as potentially subversive. This illustrates China's greatest problem – although they have embraced capitalist economic values, they still cling on to the Communist ideology when it comes to political freedom. If political unrest were to intensify in the next decade, the remarkable transformation of the Chinese economy might not continue.

AGRICULTURE IN CHINA

With such a huge population to feed, agriculture is vital to the success of the Chinese economy. Although the country has a vast land area, large parts are too mountainous or arid to produce much food. Only 11% of the land is considered to be productive. The parts of China which are cultivated for farming produce very high yields of crops. The country is the world's biggest producer of wheat crops, including rice, which is the staple food for many people. Almost 200 million tonnes of rice are produced and consumed each year.

At present China is virtually self-sufficient in food. However, unless the One Child Policy is continued and population growth reduces, then in the future China might struggle to produce enough food to feed its population.

Under Chairman Mao, communes were set up. People worked the land in return for a wage. This did not encourage them to work hard and productivity was often low. In the 1980s, the communes were broken up, and individuals were given more power.

ACTIVITIES

1 Why did China have such a backward economy in 1949?
2 What were The Four Modernisations and The Great Leap Forward?
3 Who introduced these reforms?
4 How does China's economy compare with other major countries?
5 What was the top priority for President Jiang Zemin?
6 How successful has he been?
7 Where has economic growth been concentrated?
8 In what way is China less egalitarian than it used to be?
9 How did China's economy change under Deng Xiapoing's 'to get rich is glorious' campaign?
10 What are the biggest challenges facing China's economy in the new millennium?
11 Why is China worried about the Internet?

Paddy fields being cultivated

The new system of agricultural management was called the Contract Responsibility System. The government still issued contracts to farmers, making them supply a certain amount of food each year at a fixed price. However, farmers were free to produce more if they wanted and to sell it on the open market. Most Chinese towns and villages now have markets where farmers can sell their produce. This is known as sideline production. This has greatly improved the choice and quality of food available for the Chinese people, and helped to improve rural living standards. Farmers will choose to produce products that they know will be in demand. Production of eggs and chickens, for example, has multiplied. People want these products and farmers can get a good price for them – so everyone is satisfied.

In many places farmers join together in Town and Village Enterprise groups. These are not dissimilar to the old communes, except that profit is the motive rather than sticking to the communist system. Farmers can share the cost of expensive equipment and use it on a rota basis.

One danger of the system is that some farmers become much more successful than others do. This means they can afford to buy machinery and rent larger areas of ground. Poorer farmers may give up. Total farm production continues to rise, but fewer people are working on the land. The people who have given up farming either become labourers on other farms, or they join the many others who are moving to the cities in search of work.

ACTIVITIES

1   What are the main farm products in China?
2   Why might China struggle to produce enough food in the future?
3   Describe the Contract Responsibility system.
4   Why do farmers join Town and Village Enterprise groups?
5   What is happening to the smaller, poorer farmers in China?

INDUSTRY IN CHINA

Under Mao, and also at the start of Deng's period of rule, Chinese people in towns lived under a system known as 'the Iron Rice Bowl'. Basically, people were tied to a particular industry. They were guaranteed a job for life, company housing, medical care, care when they grew old, coupons for food and clothing and so on. The state-run industry looked after, and controlled, every aspect of their life.

Deng realised that China's industries were far behind those of the rest of the world, and he wanted to keep China's place as a major world power. Change was therefore necessary. China introduced a number of reforms to its industry:

◆ The Open Door Policy encouraged foreign investment and ideas, as well as new technology. Foreign leaders were invited to China and greeted as honoured guests. Young Chinese were also encouraged to go abroad to study and to bring new ideas and technology to the country. Many joint-venture businesses were set up, with Western companies co-operating with state-run Chinese enterprises. This gave the Chinese access to Western technology and methods, and the Western companies access to cheaper production costs in China. Many well-known foreign companies are now well established in China. Everyone knows about

Chinese Special Economic Zones

McDonalds setting up in China, but other well-known names such as IBM, Motorola and even the Harvey-Nichols shopping group are now well-established.

◆ Private enterprise was encouraged. Deng recognised that private enterprise could increase overall production. It was also a way of creating jobs for China's growing population, at a time when many people were also leaving the countryside and moving to the cities. Private businesses could also be taxed, providing money for the government to subsidise state industries.

◆ People in state industries were encouraged to speak up with ideas on how things could be made more efficient. Managers were made more accountable and could be sacked if they failed to meet production targets.

SPECIAL ECONOMIC ZONES

In 1980, four Special Economic Zones were established along the eastern coast of China and included Xiamen and Shantou. Hainan Island also became a Special Economic Zone in 1988.

Features of Special Economic Zones include:

◆ incentives for foreign businesses to set up there
◆ low tax rates to encourage investment
◆ they encourage modern industries such as electronics and computer assembly
◆ most products are sold abroad
◆ low wages by western standards; high wages by Chinese standards

ACTIVITIES

1 Describe the 'Iron Rice Bowl' system.
2 What was the Open Door Policy?
3 Give examples of businesses that became involved in the Chinese economy as a result of the Open Door Policy.
4 Why was private enterprise encouraged?
5 What are the benefits of making management more accountable?
6 What are the main features of the Special Economic Zones?

THE CHINESE ENVIRONMENT

One consequence of China's economic policies has been pressure on the environment. When heavy industry was expanding in Mao's day, little or no attention was paid to protecting the environment. More recently, in the rush to catch up with the rest of the world, environmental considerations have again been ignored.

Five out of the ten most polluted cities in the world are found in China, and China is rapidly becoming the world's biggest source of air pollution. The land of the bicycle is facing stiff competition from growing numbers of cars and lorries, contributing to the problem. Most Chinese cities are blanketed in smog – a mixture of smoke and fog. Tests carried out by the World Health Organisation showed that pollution levels in northern China were ten times the recommended rate.

Coal is the major source of the pollution. Coal is China's major fuel source and is cheap and abundant. To convert China's industries to use other forms of fuel would be time-consuming and expensive. Burning coal also causes acid rain which has damaged China's forests – and those in other countries in the Far East such as Korea and Japan.

ENVIRONMENT VERSUS DEVELOPMENT

The problem lies in the low priority given to environmental issues when compared with the rapid expansion of industry and business. Two dramatic examples of this are provided by the construction of the Three Gorges Dam (Sanxiamen) on the Yangtze River and the Xialongdi Dam on the Yellow River. Both schemes have been promoted as providing great benefits for China, but little mention has been made by the authorities of the environmental costs. The schemes also give China international prestige, as they offer proof of the technological achievements possible in the country.

ACTIVITIES

1   'China has serious environmental problems.'
    What evidence is there to support this statement?
2   Why does China have such serious environmental problems?

CASE STUDY

The Three Gorges Project
The project has four aims:
◆   To control the floods of the Yangtze River. Downstream the river often floods and it is estimated that up to 300 000 people may have been killed by the Yangtze floods in the twentieth century.
◆   To produce electricity. The dam will produce huge amounts of electricity – supposedly equal to 18 nuclear power stations. This will help Chinese industry, and also provide a cleaner form of power than coal-burning power stations.
◆   To irrigate farmland. The dam will control water supply to the Yangtze Valley and delta, where over half of China's food is grown.
◆   To generate new business opportunities. The massive lake that will be created behind the Dam will be ideal for tourism, fish farming and watersports. The Chinese government see the area as a potential tourist destination.

There are also several criticisms of the project:
◆   Yangtze River sediment. The reason why the Yangtze Valley and Delta are so fertile is the sediment transported by the river. Critics believe this will clog up in the turbines on the Dam, causing the electricity supply to fail and the farmland to be deprived of its life-giving sediment.
◆   Sewage disposal. Many Chinese cities dump raw sewage into the Yangtze. Because it is a fast-flowing river, the sewage is dispersed naturally. In the future the lake behind the Dam will act as a reservoir for sewage, and the river will not flow so fast further downstream causing sewage to be deposited.
◆   Loss of land. A huge area of land will be drowned by the new lake. Not only will this mean that valuable farmland is lost, many factories will be submerged. These contain deposits of dangerous chemicals which will pollute the new lake.
◆   Population displacement. Two million people will lose their homes when the lake is created. They will have to be rehoused.
◆   Loss of historical heritage. Many important historical and archaeological sites will be submerged under the new lake.

ACTIVITY

Imagine that you are a radio reporter. You have been sent to China to produce a report on the Three Gorges Project and its impact. Write the text of your report, and make up interviews with two people – one local farmer who is to lose his land, and one businessman excited about the prospects for development.

10 HUMAN RIGHTS ISSUES IN CHINA

In this chapter you will learn about:
- ◆ political participation in China
- ◆ political dissent in China
- ◆ the Falun Gong movement
- ◆ Hong Kong
- ◆ crime, punishment and justice in China

Many protested when President Jiang Xemin visited London

HUMAN RIGHTS IN CHINA

The visit of Chinese President Jiang Xemin to Britain in October 1999 brought human rights issues into sharp focus. Jiang is said to have had a frank discussion about his country's human rights record during a meeting with Prime Minister Tony Blair. The Chinese leader raised the issue himself at the start of the talks as protesters staged a noisy protest outside Downing Street. Both he and Mr Blair are reported to have said that human rights concerns should not dominate relations between their countries. Both Britain and China preferred to concentrate on economic issues, glossing over the human rights problems.

President Jiang arrived at Downing Street via a side entrance to avoid a large protest opposite the main gates. Demonstrators were refused permission to deliver a petition to Number 10 so they pinned it to the gates outside Downing Street instead. The police took a strong line against demonstrators, dragging people away for shouting at the passing car of the Chinese President and tearing their banners from them.

President Jiang is reported to have said that his country and Britain disagreed over some human rights issues. But he added that China's record was improving. Mr Blair is said to have made it clear that Britain still had continuing concerns, but said it was important he could put them directly to Mr Jiang within the context of the deepening relationship between them.

The Prime Minister's spokesman said Mr Blair told the Chinese leader that there were also differences between them regarding Tibet. Britain favours the region being given independent control of its own affairs.

Human rights activists were unhappy that the government did not publicly put Jiang on the spot about the occupation of Tibet and human rights in China. Amnesty International campaigner Richard Bunting said: 'This is exactly what we feared: that any discussion of human rights would be confined to a hushed dialogue behind closed doors.'

Business contracts worth about £2bn between China and UK companies were confirmed at the time of the visit. Jiang also had lunch with media tycoon Rupert Murdoch to discuss business opportunities.

HUMAN RIGHTS IN CHINA – PERSONAL FREEDOM

A young dissident in Beijing recently decided to sue a senior Chinese official over what he said were untrue statements about his private life. Some weeks later, he was pleasantly surprised to see the official in question – a member of the Human Rights Institute, a government body – issue a statement of apology to the dissident for any embarrassment caused. The dispute was settled. The idea of a dissident daring to issue a court challenge against a senior official, then receiving an apology rather than punishment, is very different from the era of Mao Zedong. It is a sign of the changing times in China.

When Chairman Mao died in 1976, China was in economic ruin, ideologically bankrupt, internationally isolated and ruled by a regime whose popular support was weakening. Deng Xiaoping's solution was simple: fast economic modernisation and market liberalisation under a monolithic political system. In other words, an experiment in capitalism led by a communist party. The new approach was immortalised in his phrase: 'It doesn't matter whether a cat is black or white as long as it catches mice'. This philosophy proved popular with the Chinese people who saw great improvements in their living standards, if not in their personal freedom.

China in the 1980s and 1990s was largely dominated by two themes. First, economic success and market potential, and second, political oppression, in the shape of crackdowns on dissidents, church groups or practitioners from the Falun Gong religious sect (see page 98). But while it is important to pay attention to what is decreed from behind the walls of Zhong-nan-hai – the Forbidden City – where China's top leaders work and live, some of the biggest changes are taking place at the grass roots of Chinese society. The methods of control of people's day-to-day lives, such as the household registration system, the work-unit system and political 'brainwashing', have been greatly weakened. There is increasing separation of the state from the private life of the individual. People have more freedom and scope for basic choices in their lives than ever before – as long as they do not openly challenge the Communist Party. Their private lives are no longer the business of the state. People are no longer prosecuted or demoted for adultery. Homosexuality, condemned in the past as a social evil, is now out in the open.

At one time slavish obedience to the Party line was necessary to ensure a reasonable living standard. Now Chinese people are more worried about everyday concerns such as their children's education, health, housing, career and pension. A middle class has emerged and has increasing importance in public life.

The members of this new middle class are young or middle-aged professionals, often managers, entrepreneurs or intellectuals. They are well-educated, well-informed about the West and acutely aware

ACTIVITIES

1 Why did protesters attend the visit of Jian Xemin to Britain in 1999?

2 Why were human rights activists angry about the meetings between Jiang and Tony Blair?

3 *'The authorities have changed their response to dissidents since the days of Mao'*. What evidence is there to support this statement?

4 Explain the phrase *'It does not matter if a cat is black or white, so long as it catches mice.'*

5 What were the two themes that dominated the Chinese economy in the 1980s and 90s?

6 Who are the new Chinese Middle Class?

Karl Marx

of the problems facing China. Most of them would not go in for overt political dissent, but they are certainly not afraid of being independent or even critical of government policies in their own areas of expertise.

Typical of this new-found middle class society is the desire on the part of every major Chinese city to build its own world-class opera house. Auction houses have flourished, museum-going has become fashionable, and 'How to . . .' self-improvement books are best-sellers. These are capitalist pursuits, embraced by the newly-arrived middle class.

The Party itself has abandoned many communist policies, with the notable exception of the one-party political monopoly. Few top politicians nowadays are genuinely interested in defending Marxism. They are more bothered about specific policies than ideological goals.

POLITICAL PARTICIPATION IN CHINA

COMMUNIST IDEOLOGY

China's Communist ideology has its origin in the writings of Karl Marx, a nineteenth century German philosopher. He believed that society consisted of two groups – the proletariat (ordinary workers) and the bourgeoisie (business owners). The latter tried to exploit the former. Marx believed that it was inevitable that eventually the workers would rise up and try to overthrow the bourgeoisie, claiming their rightful share of the wealth they produced.

In their application to the real world, Marx's ideas have been altered. Lenin altered Marx's philosophy to suit the circumstances of Russia in 1917. Mao Zedong did the same in China in the 1940s. Since then Deng Xiaoping and now Jiang Xemin have made further changes to the ideology of China. They have seen the other major Communist regimes around the world swept away on a tide of change.

CHINA'S CONSTITUTION

China has a written Constitution. Amongst other things it guarantees:

> The right to vote
> The right to stand for election
> The right to freedom of speech and press
> The right to freedom of assembly
> The right to freedom of religious belief.

In practice Chinese people do not enjoy these rights.

- Almost all the candidates at elections are Communist Party candidates.
- Communist Party membership is essential if a person is to 'get on' in China. Fewer than 5% of the population are members of the Communist Party – all members are carefully vetted before they are allowed to join.
- Newspapers or broadcasters who criticise the government have been dealt with severely.
- Demonstrations have been crushed by the authorities.
- Religious sects, such as the Falun Gong, have been banned.

At grassroots level, the basic unit of social organisation is the work unit. Every Chinese person is theoretically a member of one, whether he or she works in an office, school or factory. Some Chinese now slip through the net because they work for a private company, a foreign business or are self-employed.

The work unit controls many aspects of life. It approves marriages and divorces, and in some cases even childbirth. It allocates housing, sets salaries, handles mail, recruits Party members, keeps files on every unit member, arranges transfers to jobs in other parts of the country and gives permission to travel abroad. The influence of the work unit extends to every aspect of a person's life.

THE PEOPLE'S CONGRESS SYSTEM

The Chinese Government claims that 'all power in the People's Republic of China belongs to the people.' They exercise power through the National People's Congress and the local people's congresses.

Deputies to the people's congresses at various levels are elected and are responsible to the people. The deputies are supposed to be representative of different walks of life.

In the Eighth National People's Congress, the 2978 deputies elected to serve from 1993 to 1998 were from the following backgrounds:

Occupation	Number	%
Workers	332	11.15
Farmers	280	9.4
Intellectuals	649	21.79
Cadres (civil servants)	842	28.27
Representatives of various parties	572	19.21
People's Liberation Army	267	8.97
Chinese returned from overseas	36	1.21

626, or 21.02 percent of the total, are women.

The 55 national minorities are represented by 439 deputies, making up 14.74 percent of the whole assembly.

The Chinese government claims that the country has a multi-party system. In theory the Communist Party, as the party in power, has

ACTIVITIES

1 Who 'invented' the idea of Communism?

2 Why did Marx believe that the workers would try to overthrow the bosses?

3 List the rights guaranteed by the Chinese Constitution. For each, describe how that right is treated in reality.

4 In what ways does the work unit affect a person's life?

5 Study the table on page 94 that lists the membership of the National People's Congress. Copy down the following statements and say whether each is true or false:

◆ Civil Servants are the largest group in the Congress

◆ Intellectuals outnumber the farmers and workers

◆ Other political parties have a large proportion of the places in the Congress

◆ The Chinese Army has considerable power in the Congress

◆ Women are fairly represented in the Congress

◆ National minority groups have seats in the Congress

6 What happens to opposition parties if they disagree with Communist policies?

7 Where does real political power lie?

8 What evidence is there of democracy in operation at local level in China?

ACTIVITIES

1 What was the significance of the events in Tiananmen Square in 1989?

2 Why are the Chinese government so unwilling to accept democracy?

to consult the eight other parties in the country about decisions. In practice there is no effective opposition. Other 'parties' must make their points to the Communist Party Central Committee or to local Communist Party Committees. If they do so, then they run the risk of being victimised.

The NPC is the highest body in Chinese politics. It is supposed to make laws and all important decisions on issues in national life. In theory it elects the leading personnel of the People's Republic of China, i.e. members of the Standing Committee of the NPC (the Cabinet), the President and Vice-President of the state.

However, real power lies with the Politbureau – an elite group of politicians who hold the real power. The National Congress only acts as a rubber-stamp for decisions that have already been made.

At local level there is a degree of democracy. Villages with a population of fewer than 10 000 are now allowed to elect their own leaders in free elections. This is seen by some as the beginnings of a move towards democracy in China which will spread up the political system. However, there is no sign yet that elections will spread to bigger towns and cities, and on the day that Hong Kong was returned to China the first act of the new administration was to dismiss the democratically-elected Legislative Council!

POLITICAL PROTEST IN CHINA

Although it is now a long time ago, the events of June 1989 in Tiananmen Square in Beijing are still familiar to most people. Thousands of students had occupied Tiananmen Square in support of democracy. Their protests were ended when the Chinese Army were sent in to end the demonstration. Western estimates put the death toll amongst the students at around 2000, with another 10 000 injured. The Chinese government issued a quite different set of figures, claiming only 200 had been killed.

Regardless of the true death toll, which is probably somewhere in between the two figures quoted, the events of Tiananmen Square emphasised that the Chinese government were not prepared to allow protest of this type. Economic reforms were underway by this time, but political change was simply not on the agenda for China's Communist leaders.

Martial law was imposed after Tiananmen Square and there was a major purge on opponents of the government.

So why are they so reluctant to accept democracy? Part of the answer lies in the fact that after fifty years of Communist rule, the power structure has become fixed. People within the system expect to move up when vacancies arise and they know that privileges accompany these positions of power. Secondly, some of the leaders do genuinely believe that Communism is the best system for China. They say that it has brought about great improvements in living standards, incomes and wealth, and that it would be wrong to jeopardise those gains by thinking about other political ideologies.

China – political timeline

1934	Civil War starts between the Communists and the Nationalist Government.
1949	Communists win Civil War. Mao Zedong proclaims the People's Republic of China.
1958–60	The Great Leap Forward. Mao oversees rapid growth in both industry and farming.
1966–69	The Cultural revolution – a return to strict Communist principles. Opponents of Mao wiped out.
1976	Mao dies. His wife and friends are arrested.
1978	Deng Xiaoping becomes leader of China. Introduces The Four Modernisations.
1989	Student's protest crushed at Tiananmen Square.
1997	Deng Xiaoping dies; Jiang Xemin takes over as leader.

A lone student faces a line of tanks in Tiananmen Square

DISSIDENTS

Dissidents are people who oppose the government in a totalitarian country like China. They risk arrest, imprisonment or execution. China has imprisoned many of its most vocal dissidents, while others have been forced into exile in countries such as the USA. Sometimes dissidents are taken into 'protective custody' if a foreign leader is visiting China. The idea is that this will prevent them from organising any form of demonstration that might embarrass the Chinese government.

In mid 1995 petitions calling for greater freedom of speech and an inquiry into the Tiananmen Square massacre were circulated. The intellectuals responsible for the petitions were arrested. Wang Da, a leader of the 1989 protests was re-arrested in 1996 and sentenced to 11 years in prison. Wei Jingsheng received a 14-year sentence. In 1997 two dissidents in Shenzhen (Li Wenming and Guo Baosheng) were each sentenced to three and a half years in prison. Many other dissidents are held under house arrest.

One of the difficulties with dissent in China is that there is little co-ordination. This is understandable within China, where dissidents live in constant fear of arrest. However, even those dissidents who are exiled from China have failed to organise themselves as a group. Some have given up the fight entirely. Chen Kaige, a dissident who was allowed to argue with Li Peng on television during the visit of an American politician in the 1990s, now lives in America where he runs a restaurant. Other foreign-based dissidents such as Fang Lizhi and Liu Binyan are too old to attract the attention of China's young people.

When Jing Xiamin visited London in 1999, he was upset by

dissidents who demonstrated on the streets of London. In China no such protest would have been tolerated.

ACTIVITIES

1 What are dissidents?
2 What happens to dissidents when a foreign leader visits China?
3 Describe the sentences given to some dissidents in China.
4 Why have dissidents in China not been more effective?

Hong Kong

THE RETURN OF HONG KONG

The territory of Hong Kong was a British colony on the south coast of China. It was made up of a small island, and an area of land on the mainland called the New Territories. Britain leased Hong Kong from the Chinese and knew that it would have to be handed back in 1997.

Hong Kong became an industrial and commercial centre for the whole Far East. The capitalist system made it richer than any part of China. Consequently, there were great fears as the date for returning Hong Kong to China approached. Despite guarantees that the economic system would be protected and that human rights would be respected, many people in Hong Kong feared the worst.

Those fears have been mainly unfounded. Although Hong Kong is now fully integrated with China, special political and economic freedoms have been granted and there is no sign of any loss of wealth.

TIBET

Tibet was invaded and occupied by China in 1949. It is a huge area on the north side of the Himalayan Mountains. China claims that Tibet is historically part of their land, but Tibetans themselves do not want to be part of China. The Chinese government have tried to wipe out the Tibetan culture, language and religion. Children are taught Chinese in school and only learn Tibetan at home. China has encouraged people from other parts of the country to move to Tibet. Seven and a half million have moved to Tibet, and they now outnumber the native population by almost two to one.

Tibet

The leader of Tibet's Buddhist Faith is the Dalai Lama, who was forced to flee into exile. China's leaders portray the Dalai Lama as evil, and photographs of him are banned. Since 1949, hundreds of thousands of Tibetans have been imprisoned and many have died in Chinese prisons. Tibet was the focus of demonstrations against Chinese leader Jing Xiamin when he visited London in 1999.

ACTIVITIES

1　What guarantees did Hong Kong's people want before the territory was returned to China?
2　What has happened in Hong Kong since 1997?
3　Many protesters criticise China's human rights record in Tibet. Why are they so critical of China's record in Tibet?

The Chinese authorities have tried to crack down on Falun Gong

FALUN GONG

Falun Gong, a group variously described as a cult, sect or religion, claims millions of followers around the world. The group jumped to prominence in the summer of 1999 when the Chinese government clamped down on their activities. Falun Gong followers say they are a peaceful law-abiding group, following a philosophy and regime of exercises which lead to spiritual enlightenment and improved health.

The authorities in China see Falun Gong in a far more sinister light. China banned the sect after thousands of members demonstrated in about 30 Chinese cities against the arrest of group leaders. According to state-run China TV, it is guilty of spreading fallacies, inciting disturbances and generally jeopardising social stability. In April 1999, 10 000 Falun Gong followers gathered outside the headquarters of the Communist Party in Beijing to protest about the arrest of several of their leaders.

But what is Falun Gong and why is it causing such profound unease to China's rulers? According to the group's literature, Falun Gong – or Law of the Wheel – originated in prehistoric times but only came to public notice in 1992 when Li Hongzhi, a man in his late forties referred to as 'the master', set up a study centre in Beijing. Falun Gong includes a mixture of Buddhist and Taoist beliefs; followers have a religious devotion to Master Li. Falun Gong involves the practice of a range of exercises related to the ancient Chinese art of qigong – a kind of breathing meditation.

In China, hundreds of people gather together in squares and parks throughout the country. To the accompaniment of special Falun

Gong music, they perform routines with names such as 'Buddha showing the thousand hands', 'The way of strengthening supernatural powers' and 'The Falun Gong way to heavenly circulation'.

The Zhuan Falun, the Falun Gong bible, has been translated into several languages. The Falun Gong's extensive network of websites lists movement branches in more than a dozen countries, with teaching centres in almost every major city in the USA.

It is the widespread support for Falun Gong, plus its sophisticated use of the Internet, which perhaps most alarms the Chinese authorities. Beijing has launched a campaign against the group in the official media. They are clearly frightened that Falun Gong may encourage people into more open political protest against the Communist state.

ACTIVITIES

1 What is the Falun Gong movement?
2 What are Falun Gong's main beliefs?
3 Why are the Chinese authorities opposed to Falun Gong?
4 What have the Chinese authorities done to clamp down on Falun Gong?

CHINA AND THE INTERNET

The Internet provides access to virtually unlimited information on any topic. It can be accessed from all over the world, and the information available comes from all corners of the globe. This poses a challenge for the Chinese authorities.

Until the 1980s and early 1990s, only government propaganda was available. The only other information Chinese people could get hold of were the broadcasts that people heard in secret – the Voice of America or the BBC. As recently as the late 1970s, anyone discovered listening to these stations risked a jail sentence.

Under Deng Xiaoping, Chinese people had more access to news and other information. But the real change came in the late 1990s. Technology improved, and the country had access to programmes on cable and satellite television, better telephone communication systems including cell phones, and international calls – and the Internet.

Despite the fact that Internet access is still available only in the cities, it has enjoyed spectacular success in China. Figures released in July 1999 showed that there were about four million Internet users in China. By the end of the year, numbers were expected to reach eight million.

It is possible to access information from all over the world, and perhaps more importantly, to speak to people all over the world using e-mail. Most Internet users are young male professionals with above average income, who use the Internet to find out about news and current affairs, and for entertainment. Chinese Internet users can now express themselves freely to a degree never before experienced – in a country that forbids public gatherings and demonstrations.

The Government find it difficult to control the Internet. 'You can block a demonstration with tanks, but you cannot use tanks to block the Internet,' said one Internet fan, Lian, remembering the violent suppression of the Tiananmen Square protests in June 1989.

If China is to continue to enjoy economic growth and modernisation it needs the Internet and so has invested a good deal of money in it. But the country still has a totalitarian government, and the authorities continue to exert tight control on information.

The Internet is difficult to police. Zhuhai Culture Weekly, a newspaper published in Guangdong, was closed down for publishing work by environmental journalist Dai Qing and all the staff lost their jobs. The same article was published on the Internet in the name of the same journalist with no response from the authorities.

Nevertheless, Chinese police departments have been authorised to monitor individual users of the Internet, and they can ask service providers to block troublesome web sites. A number of sites including the BBC, CNN, ABC and Voice of America have been blocked, and a Chinese computer executive who supplied e-mail addresses to a human rights organisation in the United States was sentenced to two years in prison.

The strength of the Internet was brought home to the Chinese authorities by the religious group Falun Gong. They used the Internet to spread their message, and to organise huge public demonstrations that took the government completely by surprise. When the government cracked down on the group and its leader, Li Hongzhi, it had to try to crack down on the Internet too. Many websites had been carrying material relating to the group.

Interestingly, the authorities launched their own website directed against Falun Gong – an example of the Chinese government using the new technology for their own ends, and possibly a sign of things to come.

ACTIVITIES

1 Why does the Internet present a big threat to the Chinese government?

2 How many Internet users are there in China?

3 Which Internet sites have been blocked out by the Chinese authorities?

4 What evidence is there that the Chinese government may use the Internet for their own propaganda?

CRIME AND PUNISHMENT IN CHINA

The Chinese police have extensive powers to detain people who they suspect of crimes. People can be kept in custody for up to three months without even being told why! They can be kept in prison for up to three years awaiting trial.

When trials do take place they are usually very short. It is assumed that if the police have investigated a case and brought a suspect to trial then they will be guilty. Most people plead guilty because there is a better chance of a lenient sentence. If someone pleads not guilty, and is then found guilty after a trial, the punishment is usually very severe.

THE DEATH PENALTY

The Death Penalty is used extensively in China. In 1996, it is thought that there were around 3500 executions in China – almost half of the total for the whole world. No fewer than 68 offences carry the death penalty. These include certain types of fraud, drug dealing and taking bribes, as well as crimes like murder and rape.

Execution can be carried out by shooting (usually at a public execution ground) or by lethal injection.

When prisoners are executed by shooting, they are forced to kneel on the ground with their hands tied behind them. A police officer than shoots them in the back of the head. The prisoner's family have to pay for the cost of the bullet. Often the prisoner's organs such as kidneys, heart and corneas may be used for transplants. Some human rights activists are worried that China has stepped up the number of executions to provide a bigger supply of these organs for the international market.

THE LAOGAI — LABOUR CAMPS IN CHINA

The system of prisons and labour camps in China is known as the Laogai. Prisoners in China are required to work – the belief is that they can be re-educated to stop them committing more crimes. Because they have committed a crime against the country they must work to pay for their food and accommodation in prison. Each prison or labour camp has a 'dual identity'. It is also run as a factory, with a business name indicating what it produces. Outsiders might think that Wuhan Number Three Concrete Works is a factory – in reality, it is a prison.

Conditions in China's prisons are harsh. Food is poor, buildings are damp and dirty, and anyone who steps out of line will be severely dealt with. Beatings and torture are common. Organisations like Amnesty International have described prison conditions in China as amongst the worst in the world.

ACTIVITY

Using the information above, and other sources, compile a report on Crime and Punishment in China. Use the following headings: *Crime in China, The Death Penalty, Labour Camps and Prisons in China.*

11 INTRODUCTION TO SOUTH AFRICA

In this chapter you will learn about:
◆ the provinces of South Africa
◆ the people of South Africa

Map of South Africa

Province	Western Cape
Area	129 370 sq. km
Population	4 118 000
Capital City	Cape Town
Main Industries	Clothing and textiles, printing and publishing, fishing, wine production, farming, iron and steel
Climate	Mediterranean-type climate – warm all the year round, hot and dry in summer

• One of the world's finest wine-producing areas. Many of its wines have received the highest accolades at international wine shows
• Western Cape has the lowest unemployment figures in South Africa

Province	Eastern Cape
Area	169 600 sq. km
Population	5 865 000
Capital City	Bisho
Main Industries	Motorcar manufacturing, farming
Climate	Mediterranean-type climate – warm all the year round, hot and dry in summer

• Eastern Cape has an astonishing coastline, which is a major tourist attraction
• There is a serious problem of unemployment in this region

Province	KwaZulu-Natal
Area	92 100 sq. km
Population	7 672 000
Capital City	Pietermaritzburg
Main Industries	Coal mining, sugar cane plantations, fruit farming, steel, tourism.
Climate	Sub-tropical climate. Hot and humid all year on the coast. Cold in winter on the high slopes of the Drakensberg Mountains.

- Only part of South Africa with a monarchy – special permission is given in the Constitution
- Of all the provinces, KwaZulu-Natal has the most diverse range of influences – African, British, Indian and Afrikaner

Province	Northern Cape
Area	361 830 sq. km
Population	746 000
Capital City	Kimberley
Main Industries	Diamond mining, sheep farming, horticulture, iron ore mining, copper mining, fruit and grape growing
Climate	Hot and dry in summer, cold and dry in winter

- The last remaining San (Bushmen) live in the Kalahari area of the Northern Cape
- The De Beer Diamond Company is the most important of its type in the world and has its headquarters at Kimberley

Province	Free State
Area	129 480 sq. km
Population	2 470 000
Capital City	Bloemfontein
Main Industries	Gold mining, uranium mining, coal mining, diamond mining, chemicals, wheat and grain crops
Climate	Cold and mainly dry in winter, warm and wet in summer

- Free State is the third largest province in South Africa, but has the second-smallest population
- Free State is known as the 'Granary of South Africa' because of its agricultural importance

Province	North West
Area	116 320 sq. km
Population	3 043 000
Capital City	Mafikeng
Main Industries	Gold and uranium mining, wheat production, cattle ranching, diamond mining
Climate	Savannah climate – warm in winter, hot in summer – heavy rains in summer

- Poverty is a serious problem in the rural areas of the North West
- One quarter of the labour force are employed in mining

Province	Gauteng
Area	17 010 sq. km
Population	7 171 000
Capital City	Johannesburg
Main Industries	Commerce, research, wheat crops, coal mining, manufacturing
Climate	Hot summers and cold winters. Most rainfall in summer

- Gauteng is the smallest province, but the second-most heavily populated
- Gauteng is the most urbanised and industrialised province of South Africa

Province	Mpumalanga
Area	79 490 sq. km
Population	2 646 000
Capital City	Nelspruit
Main Industries	Fruit production (especially citrus), forestry, coal mining, paper production
Climate	Hot summers and cold winters in the mountains; sub-tropical climate in the lowlands.

- Mpumalanga means 'land where the sun rises'
- Mpumalanga is one of the poorest provinces in South Africa

Province	Northern Province
Area	123 910 sq. km
Population	4 128 000
Capital City	Pietersburg
Main Industries	Cattle ranching, tropical fruit, tea and coffee, mining of coal, iron, copper and asbestos
Climate	Savannah climate. Warm in winter, hot in summer with more rainfall in summer.

- The landscape of the Northern Province is known as the Bushveld – and is ideal for cattle ranching
- This province has most in common with developing African nations to the North – it has good communication links to Maputo in Mozambique

STATISTICS ABOUT THE REGIONS

Urban and Rural Population (%)

	Urban	Rural
South Africa	55.4	44.6
Western Cape	89.9	10.1
Eastern Cape	37.3	62.7
Northern Cape	71.7	28.3
Free State	69.6	30.4
KwaZulu Natal	43.5	56.5
North West	34.8	65.2
Gauteng	96.4	3.6
Mpumalanga	37.3	62.7
Northern Province	11.9	88.1

Human Development Index is a measure of how well developed an area is. It includes measures of quality of life, basic amenities, income levels etc.

Life Expectancy At Birth (Years) – 1991

Area	Life Expectancy
South Africa	62.7
Western Cape	67.7
Eastern Cape	60.7
Northern Cape	62.7
Free State	61.9
KwaZulu Natal	61.6
North West	59.7
Gauteng	66.0
Mpumalanga	62.4
Northern Province	62.5

Human Development Index – 1991

Area	HDI
South Africa	0.677
Western Cape	0.826
Eastern Cape	0.607
Northern Cape	0.698
Free State	0.657
KwaZulu Natal	0.602
North West	0.543
Gauteng	0.818
Mpumalanga	0.691
Northern Province	0.470

Pupil/Teacher Ratio in Schools 1995

Area	P/T Ratio
South Africa	33.7
Western Cape	25.7
Eastern Cape	41.3
Northern Cape	27.2
Free State	34.6
KwaZulu Natal	35.6
North West	30.3
Gauteng	28.1
Mpumalanga	36.1
Northern Province	36.6

Adult Literacy By Province (%)

Area	
South Africa	82.2
Western Cape	94.6
Eastern Cape	72.3
Northern Cape	79.8
Free State	84.4
KwaZulu Natal	84.3
North West	69.5
Gauteng	92.9
Mpumalanga	75.5
Northern Province	73.6

ACTIVITIES

Compare the regions of South Africa in terms of each of the following categories.

Remember that when you are comparing things you should look for similarities and differences.

◆ area
◆ population
◆ main industries
◆ rural/urban population
◆ language spoken
◆ life expectancy
◆ Human Development Index
◆ pupil/teacher ratio
◆ adult literacy

THE PEOPLE OF SOUTH AFRICA

Population – by ethnic group (%)

Ethnic Group	1970	1980	1985	1991	1994	1995
Africans	70.6	72.5	73.7	75.3	76.0	76.3
Coloureds	9.5	9.2	9.0	8.7	8.6	8.5
Indians	2.9	2.8	2.7	2.6	2.6	2.5
Whites	16.9	15.5	14.7	13.4	12.8	13.7

Life Expectancy At Birth – by population group

Ethnic Group	1980	1991
All Groups	58.8	62.8
Africans	56.2	60.3
Coloureds	58.5	66.5
Indians	65.3	68.9
Whites	70.4	73.1

Average Annual Population Growth Rates (%)

Ethnic Group	1970 –1980	1980 –1991	1991 –1995	1970 –1995
Total	2.52	2.47	2.06	2.40
Africans	2.78	2.78	2.40	2.72
Coloureds	2.19	1.90	1.43	1.94
Indians	2.31	1.78	1.40	1.93
Whites	1.58	1.07	0.67	1.21

Main Source of Domestic Water (%)

Ethnic Group	Running tap-water in dwelling	Running tap-water on site	Tap-water from communal tap	Borehole or well	River/dam/spring	Other
All Groups	51.4	20.2	11.1	7.1	9.8	0.5
Africans	32.7	27.3	15.6	9.6	14.0	0.7
Coloureds	72.2	20.0	4.7	0.9	1.9	0.2
Indians	96.8	1.2	0.7	0	0	0
Whites	96.9	0.3	0.4	2.0	0.4	0

Mean Years of Schooling – by population group

Ethnic Group	1980	1991
All Groups	5.43	6.86
Africans	3.63	5.53
Coloureds	5.72	6.94
Indians	6.98	8.78
Whites	10.96	11.67

Unemployment – by population group

1994	1995
32.6	29.3
41.1	36.9
23.3	22.3
17.1	13.4
6.4	5.5

Percentage of households owning a television

1994	1996
41.9	48.3
N/A	N/A
81.3	84.0
95.8	96.0
95.7	96.5

ACTIVITIES

Compare the different population groups in South Africa in terms of each of the following categories.

Remember to look for similarities and differences when making comparisons.

- changes in population composition since 1970
- population growth
- changes in life expectancy
- main source of domestic water
- average number of years of schooling
- changes in unemployment rate
- percentage of households owning a television

12 THE HISTORY OF SOUTH AFRICA

Discoveries at Taung and other sites in the country bear witness to the fact that prehistoric man lived about one and a half million years ago in what is today known as South Africa. These people were nomadic. The San were the first people to settle permanently. About 2000 years ago, the Khoikhoi who settled in the Western Cape followed them.

The first Europeans to reach the Cape of Good Hope, toward the end of the fifteenth century, were Portuguese explorers seeking a sea route to the east. The explorer Vasco da Gama landed in South Africa, but showed little interest in the Khoikhoi natives – he was more concerned about finding his new route to India. The Dutch East India Company established the first permanent European settlement in 1652. Jan Van Riebeeck founded a colony at Cape Town where he set up farms to produce animals and vegetables to supply ships stopping en-route to the Dutch colonies of the East Indies. By 1688, some 800 farmers were settled around the Cape, and they came into increasing conflict with the local Khoikhoi.

Some of the Dutch settlers resented the fact that they were obliged to hand over all their produce to the Dutch East India Company, who paid them a wage. Some of the Boers (farmers) set up their own colony further inland, separate from Dutch control. This brought them into closer contact and conflict with native peoples.

By the middle of the eighteenth century, the growing colony came into contact with the African tribes that were established in the southeast coastal regions and expanding south-westward. Between 1770 and 1840 there were seven different wars against the Xhosa people.

In 1806, the British established themselves in Cape Town. Dutch colonial influence was weakening by that time, and Britain was taking over as the major world colonial power. They also saw Cape Town as a convenient staging post for supplying ships on their way to the far-flung corners of the British Empire such as Australia and India.

The British colonists were prepared to trade with the Africans and treated them well. This caused a rift with the Boers, who began calling themselves Afrikaners to distinguish themselves from the more recently arrived colonists.

The first decades of the nineteenth century were filled with wars between the black nations, resulting in the emergence of the Zulu nation under Shaka (and later Dingaan) as the dominant power in KwaZulu/Natal.

The fighting between different African groups left a vacuum in central South Africa. This was filled in 1834 when some 14 000 Boers migrated inland from the Cape, in what was known as the Great Trek. They were fed up with life at the Cape and the attitude of the British and wanted to establish their own separate colony. The Afrikaners established the states of Transvaal in 1852, and the Orange Free State in 1854. These areas were already occupied by some African groups, who put up violent opposition to the incomers.

The British accepted the new Boer colonies. At the time they were established, the interior of South Africa was regarded as a worthless area, and the Boers provided a buffer between the British and possible attacks from Africans.

Conflict between the Boers and the British erupted in the late nineteenth century when valuable gold and diamond reserves were discovered in the interior. The first valuable deposits were uncovered in 1866. Britain proposed a federation between the Cape Colony, Transvaal, Natal and the Orange Free State. The proposal was rejected by the Boers and in 1899 war broke out.

Britain had the backing of its huge Empire, while the Boers were given support by Germany. After three years of war, in which 50 000 people died and over 100 000 Boers were confined in British concentration camps, the Boers surrendered and accepted British domination.

The Boers' attitude towards the Africans was that they were little more than savages. The Boers approved of slavery. The British were slightly more enlightened. They opposed slavery because the Africans could be buyers in a market economy, increasing the wealth of the British. This did not stop the British from discriminating against the Africans in economic and social terms. The British also brought in outside labour from Mozambique, Lesotho, Botswana and India. Migrant workers were not allowed to bring their families with them, and had to leave the country if they lost their job.

In 1910 the Cape Colony and Natal (British) and the Orange Free State and Transvaal (Boer republics) were joined to form the Union of South Africa under the leadership of Boer generals Louis Botha and Jan Smuts. The Act of Union was followed by a resurgence of Afrikaner nationalism. The rights of Africans were ignored in the Constitution of the Union of South Africa.

After 1910 segregation increased. The 1913 Natives Land Act set aside 7% of South Africa for Africans, and it became home to 35% of the country's population. Much of the remaining land was reserved for whites, who represented only 20% of the population. In the African areas, subsistence farming was the only means of livelihood. The white areas were intensively farmed, with African labour used as a cheap source of production.

Nationally organised political activity among Africans began with the establishment of the African National Congress (ANC) in 1912. In 1959 the Pan African Congress (PAC) was founded as a breakaway from the ANC because of its dissatisfaction with the non-racist policies of the ANC. Meanwhile restrictions were placed on the movements of Africans and Indians and they were prohibited from acquiring title to land in 1913, although certain territories were reserved for black tribal ownership. African voters were removed from the common role in 1936.

The Afrikaner nationalist movement grew steadily. Through the Afrikaner Broederbond – a sort of secret society – Afrikaners gained great influence in the control of industry and politics. Afrikaners resented their loss of power and influence to the British after the Boer War, and many were forced to become workers in mining and industry. This led to the re-emergence of Afrikaner nationalism in the form of the National Party, who under Dr. D F Malan, won the post-war election in 1948. At the time a slogan of the National Party was 'Gevaar KKK', meaning 'Beware – Kafir (Blacks), Koelie (Indians) and Komunism (Communism).

ACTIVITIES

1   Which groups were the original inhabitants of South Africa?
2   Why did both the Dutch and the British set up colonies at the Cape?
3   Compare the attitudes of the British and Dutch settlers towards the native South Africans.
4   Why did the Dutch set off on the Great Trek?
5   Why did conflict erupt between the British and the Boers?
6   'Apartheid began in 1913.' What evidence is there to support this statement?
7   Why was the ANC formed?
8   What was the significance of the Broederbond?

1948 ONWARDS – THE IMPOSITION OF APARTHEID

In the election campaign of 1948, Malan's National Party promised to look after the interests of white South Africans. The National Party swept to power and Malan was able to implement one of his main election promises – the policy of apartheid.

Apartheid, which literally means 'separateness', was really a policy of racial segregation. Black and White were to have separate provisions in every aspect of life – different schools, living areas, leisure facilities and so on. Prior to 1948 the rights of Black South Africans had been limited – after 1948 they were removed completely under the system of Apartheid.

The first step in the creation of the apartheid system was to define the races or national groups to which people belonged. This was done through the *Population Registration Act (1950)*. All people in South Africa were classified as belonging to one of four racial groups – White, Coloured, Indian or African. The *Pass Laws (1952)* required all people to carry a Pass Book that contained their photograph and details of their racial group. These laws meant that the authorities could dictate who was where at any given time. If a person did not have a pass book then at best they would be fined, and at worst, they would be sent to another part of the country.

Having defined the population in these terms, the purity of the racial groups could be maintained through the enforcement of the *Mixed Marriages Act (1950)*. This banned inter-marriage between different groups, and the position was strengthened by the *Immorality Act (1950)* which banned inter-racial sexual relations of any kind.

During the 1950s, the South African government developed the Homelands policy. This was a way of answering allegations from the outside world that the apartheid system denied basic human rights to the Black South Africans, who made up the majority of the population. The government looked at the map of South Africa and identified 'tribal homelands' or Bantustans. These were mainly areas with minimal economic value – poor quality agricultural land, and no minerals of any significance. The idea was that Blacks would be made citizens of these 'independent homelands', although they would need to remain living in South Africa as 'foreign guests' in order to obtain work. This policy was gradually implemented through a number of acts including the *Bantu Authorities Act (1951), Promotion of Bantu Self Government Act (1959)* and the *Bantu Homelands Citizenship Act (1970)*. The Bantustans were never viable economic units, some of them consisting of ten or more separate parcels of land. No government apart from South Africa ever recognised them as independent nations, yet when Transkei (1976) and Boputhatswana (1977) became 'independent', South Africa championed this as a triumph of human rights. The fact was that many of the citizens of these 'new countries' had never even seen their homeland let alone lived there – they were housed in the vast townships on the edge of South Africa's main cities.

The South African government enforced the apartheid system through a number of security laws which were designed to stamp out all opposition to the system. It is a measure of how successful they were that for over 40 years the apartheid system endured, despite the fact that Blacks made up three-quarters of the South African population.

The *Suppression of Communism Act (1950)* outlawed the Communist Party and a whole range of political beliefs. These were not what outsiders would have described as Communism – they included any form of organised opposition to the apartheid system. Under this act, the authorities had powers to:
◆ ban people from particular places or areas
◆ place people under house arrest
◆ prevent people from receiving visitors
◆ ban people from attending any public events, including funerals
◆ sack people from 'sensitive' jobs such as teaching.

In 1976 the Suppression of Communism Act was renamed the *Internal Security Act*.

The *Unlawful Organisations Act (1960)* was originally intended to ban the African National Congress (ANC) and the Pan African Congress (PAC). The powers of the Act were extended to allow the authorities to ban any organisation which they thought was organising protest against the system.

The *Terrorism Act (1967)* defined terrorism as 'any act designed to endanger or overthrow state authority'. The punishment was death. Anyone arrested under this act could be detained indefinitely for questioning, and their families were not informed that they were in custody. Some people were detained 'for questioning' for over a year, by which time their families believed them to be dead.

In 1982 all the previous acts were combined into a new *Internal Security Act*. This gave the authorities total freedom to arrest and detain people for a variety of reasons, including subversion and incitement. If the police thought someone might be protesting or organising protest, peaceful or violent, then they could be arrested and detained without charge.

The South African police and defence forces were well equipped to deal with protest. The weapons at their disposal ranged from sjamboks (rhino-skin whips), to water cannons, CS Gas, rubber bullets, shotguns and live ammunition. They were all used to disperse protesters.

ACTIVITIES

1 Why was the 1948 general Election so important?
2 Define apartheid.
3 Give a brief description of the:
   a) Population Registration Act
   b) Pass Laws
   c) Mixed Marriages Act
   d) Immorality Act
4 What was the aim behind the establishment of the Bantu Homelands?
5 Which organisations were banned under the Unlawful Organisations Act?
6 What were the main provisions of the Internal Security Act (1982)?

LIFE UNDER THE APARTHEID SYSTEM

For many Black and Coloured South Africans the homelands policy was nothing more than a sham. They remained in South Africa itself because they formed the labour force which supported the economy. Black workers did most of the work in the mines and in the service type jobs in the big cities (cleaners, waiting staff etc.).

Under apartheid, land was divided up for the different racial groups. Residential areas were set aside for each group – Black, Coloured and White. This was done under the notorious *Group Areas Act (1950)*. Establishing these areas led to many families being uprooted and forced to move to new areas. Most of those who moved were Blacks and Coloureds who were forced out of White areas. Blacks and Coloureds were usually allocated areas on the edges of towns and cities, with the nicest areas being reserved for the Whites. Black people were also prevented from owning businesses in designated White areas. As the White areas usually included city centres, this made it difficult for Blacks to run a successful business of any kind. Some 84% of the land was allocated to Whites, Coloured and Indians. Within that area, 99% was preserved for Whites with only 1% for Indians and Coloureds.

The Stallard Principle, first expressed in 1922 stated that:
'Blacks are permitted in the White homeland to do work that is there for them to do and not because they have equal claim to that of the Whites for presence there. The converse applies to Whites in Black Homelands.'

This principle was applied through the *Black (Urban Areas) Consolidation Act*, which controlled the movement of Blacks into White areas. All Blacks were registered as citizens of an independent homeland, but they were allowed to stay in White South Africa provided that they had a job, or were the wife or dependent child of someone working in South Africa. In that case, they were permitted to live in one of the designated Black areas, usually outside the town or city boundaries. This led to the formation of the massive black townships around every South African city, the most famous of

Soweto township

which is Soweto (South West Township) outside Johannesburg. Black people who really did come from the homelands and wanted to work in South Africa were given 11-month 'passes' as migrant workers. They were not allowed to bring their families with them, seeing them only when they returned for their one-month 'leave'. Their families could visit them in South Africa, but only with a '72 hour pass', and the journey involved was too long and expensive for most. Migrant workers lived in single-sex hostels in the black areas near their work.

Soweto is home to more than one million people. Under the apartheid system, the quality of education and health care was terrible. Every morning there was a huge exodus of people by bus and train into Johannesburg to work – by dusk everyone had to return, as to remain in the White areas after dark was a criminal offence. Housing is mainly rented from the council and is overcrowded – an average of six people per home.

Alexandria is a township for single-sex hostel dwellers on the edge of Johannesburg. It contains 24 massive housing blocks which are home to 60 000 migrant workers for eleven-months of the year. Living conditions here are basic – four people per room, one toilet for every four rooms, one shower for every nine rooms. In such conditions it is little wonder that alcoholism, drug abuse, crime and mental illness reached high levels.

Soweto and Alexandria were legitimate settlements under the apartheid system. Crossroads, a squatter camp on the edge of Cape Town, was an illegal camp where people were prepared to ignore the law in order to maintain family life. Crossroads developed as an illegal alternative to the single-sex hostels of the likes of Alexandria, where migrant workers and their families lived together in defiance of the laws. The authorities largely turned a blind eye to such camps.

Under apartheid some people were forced out of their homes and made to go and live in homelands. If Black settlements existed in White areas then the people were removed and the dwellings razed to the ground in a form of 'ethnic cleansing'. The breadwinner would be given the chance of a job and a place in a hostel – their family would be sent off to live in a homeland.

The physical segregation involved in apartheid applies to all aspects of life. The *Reservation of Separate Amenities Act (1953)* allowed for the reservation of public places and vehicles for the exclusive use of people belonging to a specific race. Distribution was not equal. The *Liquor Act (1928, amended 1977)* prevented the consumption of alcohol by different races in the same premises. The *Motor Transport Act (1955)* imposed segregation in buses and taxis, by requiring them to display a sign saying 'Whites Only' or 'Non Whites'. The *State Aided Institutions Act (1957)* laid down different opening hours or days of opening for different racial groups at libraries, museums art galleries and zoos. These laws were collectively known as 'Petty Apartheid'.

In July 1985, the government declared a State of Emergency in certain parts of South Africa. This was extended to the whole country in 1986 and lasted until 1990. Under the State of Emergency, the authorities had the power to:

◆ impose curfews
◆ censor the news media
◆ arrest and detain suspects without warrant
◆ interrogate prisoners without the presence of lawyers
◆ seal off curfew areas to all but the armed forces.

The reasons for imposing the State of Emergency were as follows:

◆ To prevent demonstrations to mark the Tenth Anniversary of the Soweto uprising. Scare stories in the White press said that Blacks were about to extend terror tactics to White areas.
◆ Increasing support for extreme right-wing parties. In particular, the Afrikaner Weerstandsbeweging (AWB) was growing in power, and Prime Minister Botha sought to appease these groups by taking direct action.
◆ The government was heavily influenced by the military. Botha's advisers suggested a military solution to the country's problems of disorder.

ACTIVITIES

1 Describe the provisions of the Group Areas Act?
2 What was the Stallard Principle?
3 Describe conditions in townships such as Soweto and Alexandra.
4 What powers did the government have under the 1985 State of Emergency?

ACTIVITY

Imagine you were an Afrikaner in the mid 1980s. In no more than 150 words, justify the policy of apartheid.

JUSTIFICATION OF APARTHEID

The Afrikaner-dominated government, supported by the majority of Whites in South Africa from 1948 until the early 1990s, justified apartheid on a number of grounds:

◆ The fact that South Africa was made up of such a diverse range of racial groups, each with their own history and culture.
◆ The strong nationalist culture in each racial group.
◆ The established 'nationhood' of White South Africans – they had colonised an 'empty area' after the Great Trek.
◆ Apartheid prevents inter-racial conflict as witnessed in the USA and UK.
◆ Apartheid allows the Bantustans to plan and develop their own identity to meet the wishes of their people.
◆ Apartheid protects the economic wealth of the White South Africans.
◆ South Africa was a pillar against the spread of communism in Africa.

INTERNAL OPPOSITION TO APARTHEID

Black opposition to Apartheid is listed in the following chronology

1912	Formation of the African National Congress (ANC)
1949	ANC adopts Programme of Action

1952	Launching of Defence Campaign against Unjust Laws by the ANC and Indian Congress
1955	Formation of South African Congress of Trades Unions (COSATU)
1956	20 000 women march against the extension of the pass laws
1959	Establishment of the Pan African Congress
1960	Sharpeville – massacre of peaceful demonstrators by the police
1961	ANC Military Wing 'Spear of the Nation' takes first action after ANC and PAC are banned
1962	Nelson Mandela visits other countries for military training
1967	ANC and ZAPU take joint action against White regime in Rhodesia
1973	Strikes by Black workers
1976	Soweto Uprising
1980	Campaign for release of Mandela; boycott of education system
1984–87	Countrywide riots and demonstrations
1988	Church Leaders and some newspapers defy censorship laws to speak out.

Gradually the internal opposition began to wear down the resistance of the White people and the government. The methods used by Black organisations can be summarised as:
◆ military action
◆ boycotts of elections, schools, shops
◆ strikes
◆ mass demonstrations
◆ violence against Black collaborators (terrorises the Black community into cooperation)
◆ diplomatic and political links with foreign states and sympathetic organisations (e.g. Anti-Apartheid Movement in the UK).

The most significant groups in the war against Apartheid were:
◆ *The African National Congress.* Formed in 1912, the ANC campaigned on a purely peaceful platform until the early 1960s. Its leader from 1952 until 1960, Chief Albert Luthuli, was a dignified activist and reformer, similar in style to Martin Luther King. After the Sharpeville massacre, the ANC, now banned, became an underground organisation, led by Nelson Mandela. He was sentenced to life imprisonment in 1964, for planning a series of explosions against economic targets such as power lines. By this time the ANC had a military wing – Umkhonto We Sizwe (Spear of the Nation). Banned in South Africa, the ANC operated from the so-called 'front line states' – Angola, Zambia and Mozambique in particular. They received arms and training from the Soviet bloc. As well as organising 'terrorism-style' attacks, they also organised political opposition to the apartheid regime.

◆ *Pan African Congress*. Split from the ANC in the late 1950s. The ANC believed in equal rights for all South Africans, Black and White. The PAC supported an all-African South Africa with no place for the White community.

◆ *Trade Unions*. The Federation of South African Trade Unions (FOSATU) and the South African Allied Workers Union (SAAWU), fought on non-racial grounds for basic human rights and greater rights for workers. The National Union of Mineworkers, then led by Cyril Ramaphosa, won concessions for Black miners in the 1970s. Wage differentials between Black and White miners were reduced from 20:1 to 5:1. In 1985, the main Trade Unions combined to form COSATU (Confederation of South African Trade Unions). During the State of Emergency COSATU organised significant opposition to the apartheid regime.

◆ *South African Students Organisation (SASO)*. Campaigned for equal rights in education, and organised protests amongst students.

◆ *Black Consciousness*. Founded mainly through SASO, this group tried to make black people proud of their racial group and traditions. Their leader, Steve Biko, died in police custody in September 1977.

◆ *The United Democratic Front*. Following the banning of the ANC and the PAC, the UDF became an 'umbrella organisation' for local community rights groups and civic associations.

◆ *Church Leaders*. When all political opposition was banned, then church leaders were often the only people who could speak out against the apartheid system. The government could not be seen to clamp down on religious leaders for fear of greater international condemnation. In the 1970s two men, Bishop Desmond Tutu and Dr Alan Boesak emerged as voices who spoke out against the system and won respect worldwide.

Archbishop Desmond Tutu

ACTIVITIES

1 Which organisations were involved in opposition to Apartheid?
2 What methods were used to oppose Apartheid within South Africa?
3 What was the reason for the split between the ANC and the PAC?
4 Who were:
   a) Albert Luthuli
   b) Nelson Mandela
   c) Cyril Ramaphosa
   d) Steve Biko
   e) Desmond Tutu?

EXTERNAL OPPOSITION TO APARTHEID

South Africa's extraordinary economic circumstances made external reaction to the apartheid system difficult to predict. While many countries were morally offended by apartheid, they could not afford to sever links with South Africa, so they grew to tolerate the system.

The USA was in a particularly difficult situation during the Cold War. South Africa was a defence against Communism, but the apartheid system was offensive to the principles of democracy. President Reagan was reluctant to impose trade sanctions on South Africa, but Congress overruled him. In 1986, comprehensive sanctions were applied which would only be lifted if South Africa made major steps towards democracy. There was an almost total trade ban on the South Africans, and American advisers and investment were withdrawn. President Bush lifted the sanctions in 1991.

South Africa left the British Commonwealth in 1961. Under Margaret Thatcher Britain had the same approach as America under President Reagan, called constructive engagement. The British government was concerned about the loss of British investments in South Africa, but the opposition parties campaigned for sanctions. Britain was forced to take some sanctions when the Commonwealth agreed to them in 1985. At the Commonwealth Summit in 1989, Britain was outvoted 48–1 by the other Commonwealth countries who wanted to escalate sanctions. Britain removed all sanctions against South Africa in 1991.

Trade sanctions did have a serious effect on South Africa, although as time went on South African industry became more self-sufficient and reliant. However, the ban on direct investment in South Africa had a greater effect, and the economy lagged behind that of other major countries.

Groups such as the Anti-Apartheid Movement tried to make sure that consumers around the world were aware of South African produce, and tried to get people to boycott it. As a result, sales of South African fruit (exported through the government-run Outspan organisation) and wine slumped, only to recover in the 1990s after major political changes.

The United Nations allowed South Africa to retain membership during the apartheid years, but refused to allow the government delegation to take its seat in the General Assembly. The UN members stated that the delegation was not representative of the South African people. Instead, they recognised the ANC as the legitimate voice of the South African people.

South Africa was isolated from world sport. Because teams were not selected on the grounds of ability, they were not allowed to compete against other countries and were suspended or expelled by most of the major sporting organisations. Athletes and other sportsmen from around the world were sometimes lured to South Africa to compete, but they were subsequently disciplined and some were banned from all competition.

The combined effects of international sanctions and internal pressure from the unrest put considerable pressure on the South African government, and the forces for change took hold.

MODERNISING APARTHEID (1979–1988)

In 1976, there seemed little prospect of change in South Africa. Prime Minister Vorster, speaking after the massacres in Soweto, said: *'When our survival is at stake, no rules apply'.*

Vorster retired in 1978 to be replaced by PW Botha. Both introduced reforms in an attempt to create 'apartheid with a human face'. There was no way that he intended to go as far as giving the Blacks rights such as the vote, but he was prepared to relax some of the laws concerning petty apartheid. This policy appeared to win few friends. The extremist

ACTIVITIES

1 Why was the USA reluctant to take action against South Africa?
2 What was 'constructive engagement'?
3 How effective were trade sanctions against South Africa?
4 What methods did the worldwide Anti-Apartheid Movement use?
5 In what ways was South Africa isolated from the rest of the world?

The aftermath of the Soweto massacre

ACTIVITIES

1 Describe the reforms introduced by PW Botha.
2 What was Desmond Tutu's reaction to these reforms?
3 Compare the policies of the Conservative Party and the National Party towards apartheid in the 1980s.

right-wing Afrikaners called him a 'Kaffitbotie', or 'Nigger Brother'. Bishop Desmond Tutu, speaking for the Blacks said:
'We do not want apartheid to be liberalised – we want it abolished'.

Botha was keen to improve South Africa's image in the international community. He also believed that creating a black middle class would split the Black community down the middle, and allow the Whites to retain supremacy. In 1983 Botha introduced a new constitution. On paper, it gave some political power to Coloureds and Asians, although Blacks were still excluded. In practice, White supremacy was still total despite the constitutional changes. Botha was now known as President Botha rather than Prime Minister as a result of the changes.

Although there was relaxation of the laws of petty apartheid, unrest and disorder amongst Blacks escalated. In 1984 there was trouble in Sharpeville and Uitenhage which led to the establishment of the State of Emergency. Botha stopped the reform process as he sought to regain control of the country. Strict censorship laws were applied and many foreign journalists were expelled from South Africa – the BBC's Michael Buerk was one who spoke out against the system and found himself on a plane home to Britain.

At local council elections in the mid 1980s the Conservative Party had considerable success, defeating the National Party in many places. Town councils re-imposed petty apartheid laws as local 'by laws', and the situation appeared to be getting worse.

DISMANTLING APARTHEID (1989–1991)

President Botha was taken ill in January 1989 and replaced as President by FW De Klerk. The General Election of September 1989 was to prove crucial to the future of South Africa. Blacks were as usual excluded from the voting, but Coloureds and Asians were able to vote. Pre-election speculation was that the National Party was about to lose their 41-year grip on power, as opposition came from both left and right. The Conservative Party spoke for the Afrikaners who were totally opposed to change, while the Democratic Party represented those who did want change – including many Coloureds, Indians and descendants of the 'Anglos'. In the event, the National Party retained their majority in the House of Assembly, and De Klerk interpreted this as a mandate for further reforms.

He opened a dialogue with Black leaders, allowed protest marches in major cities, and released some ANC prisoners from jail, including some who had been jailed along with Nelson Mandela in the early 1960s. President de Klerk met with Mandela in late 1989 to discuss the possibility of his release.

This paved the way for the massive changes that took place in 1990:

◆ On February 2nd 1990, De Klerk announced that the ANC and

FW de Clerk

Nelson Mandela after being released from jail

other Black nationalist movements would be legalised immediately.

◆ He also announced that Nelson Mandela would be released from prison on February 11th, and that the death penalty would not be carried out on any prisoners currently on 'death row'.

The far right were outraged. The Conservative Party organised a series of demonstrations, and the AWB sent a column of para-military supporters into Pretoria chanting 'Hang De Klerk, Hang Mandela'.

De Klerk was not deflected from his purpose and further reforms went ahead:

◆ In May 1990 the ANC and the government held their first face-to-face talks and agreed to negotiate a new non-racial constitution.

◆ In June 1990 De Klerk suspended the State of Emergency in all areas except Natal, where fighting between rival Black factions was a serious problem.

◆ In August 1990, the ANC agreed to suspend its armed struggle. The National Party changed its own rules to permit Black members.

◆ By February 1991, the Group Areas Act and the Population Registration Act were repealed.

Preparations were made for negotiating a new constitution for South Africa. The National Party and the ANC were to be the main contributors, but all shades of opinion were allowed to be represented at the talks. The Convention for a Democratic South Africa (CODESA) began in December 1991.

ACTIVITY

Describe five major changes made by FW De Klerk.

REASONS FOR CHANGE

It is important to understand the reasons why De Klerk instigated change in South Africa. Most observers were staggered by the speed and the scale of the changes brought about – even Desmond Tutu said 'he has taken my breath away'. Only a few years earlier, when the State of Emergency was at its height and repression at its peak, the prospects for change in South Africa looked very bleak indeed.

The reasons for the changes can be summarised as follows:

◆ The 1989 election manifesto of the National Party had offered the electorate a programme for future reform. For this reason, the election result gave De Klerk the mandate he wanted. The combined strength of the National and Democratic Parties (126 MPs) totally outweighed the Conservatives (33 MPs). De Klerk's new style of leadership had rekindled support for reform and apartheid was seen now as a policy for the far right only.

◆ Even within the Afrikaner community, the demand for reform was intensifying. The leader of the Dutch Reformed Church, to which most Afrikaners belonged, dropped its demands that the ANC renounce all violence as a precondition to negotiations.

Surprisingly, the Broederbond also dropped its opposition to change – saying that Black majority rule would not necessarily mean an end to Afrikaner culture – all racial groups could co-exist in a new South Africa.

◆ Sanctions and isolation from the world economy were beginning to have a serious effect on South Africa. In particular the lack of foreign investment meant that South Africa was in an economic recession. The White business community had long supported reform – they knew that South Africa needed to be on the world stage, and also felt that if the hopes and wishes of Black people were met then they would form a whole new group of potential customers to develop the economy.

◆ Under Botha the military had become very powerful in South Africa. They favoured White supremacy and could impose it by force. Botha's illness allowed De Klerk to manoeuvre the military chiefs out of positions of power. Many White South Africans had never really supported what was effectively a military dictatorship.

◆ Changes in the rest of the world affected South Africa. Communism was no longer a threat with the collapse of the USSR and Eastern Europe. The ANC would be bargaining from their own position, not from that of spreading world communism. Changes in countries like Mozambique and Angola suggested that Black activists could form democratic and stable governments.

ACTIVITY

Explain the five reasons why De Klerk made these changes. Use your own words where possible.

THE INTERIM CONSTITUTION

In September 1991 the government, the ANC, the Inkatha Freedom Party (IFP) and a range of other organisations committed themselves to peace and laid the foundations of the CODESA talks, aimed at creating a non-racial, democratic South Africa. Central to CODESA was the concept of power-sharing which would provide strong regional government, and meet the demands of some of the right-wingers.

The talks were delayed by outbreaks of violence between the ANC supporters and Inkatha supporters in the province of KwaZulu-Natal. Inkatha was the party of the Zulus, while the ANC represented the other Black population groups. Inkatha was fearful that they might be excluded from any settlement and they did their best to disrupt the talks. Allegations emerged that Inkatha was being funded and armed by factions within the White government with the specific aim of disrupting the peace process. The ANC finally withdrew from the CODESA talks in June 1992 after the massacre of some of their supporters by IFP activists at Boipatong.

As violence escalated and the likelihood of civil war grew, the government and the ANC resumed bi-lateral talks, quite separate from the CODESA procedures. The government under De Klerk still had a mandate for further reform, following a referendum in March 1992 which resulted in a 68% vote in favour of reform based on an 85% turnout of Whites. In February 1993 the ANC and the government agreed that multi-party elections should take place early in 1994. The Multi-Party Negotiating Forum (MPNF), which had taken the place of CODESA, finally set the election date for April 27th 1994.

Under the terms of the Interim Constitution, South Africa was to be divided into nine provinces with each responsible for things like education, law and order and taxation. National issues such as economic policy and security would be determined at central government level. The idea was that the provinces could reflect the particular population groups – especially Inkatha in Natal, as well as the Afrikaners.

The new Parliament was to consist of two chambers, the National Assembly (made up of 400 members – 200 elected by proportional representation from national lists, and 200 from provincial lists) and the Senate (comprised of 90 members, 10 to be elected by each of the nine provinces).

A joint sitting of the National Assembly and the Senate would be know as the Constituent Assembly and would have responsibility for drafting South Africa's permanent constitution. The Interim Constitution provided for the President of South Africa to be elected at the first sitting of the National Assembly. All parties with at least 20% of the seats in the National Assembly were to be able to nominate a Vice president. The Cabinet was to be made up of no more than 27 ministers, with each party holding more than 20 seats being entitled to representation in the Cabinet according to size. The Interim Constitution made it clear that the government was to think in terms of national consensus rather than individual party needs – a clear indication that there was an awareness of the possible consequences of political instability.

The Interim Constitution included a Bill of Rights detailing basic rights granted to all South African citizens. These included freedom of speech, equality before the law and the right to strike. Finally, an Independent Electoral Commission (IEC) was set up to supervise the 1994 General Election and ensure that they were free and fair.

The Afrikaner Volksfront, an umbrella organisation for Afrikaner parties including the Conservative Party and the AWB, were not involved in approving the Interim Constitution. Neither were Inkatha, who were deeply suspicious of the ANC. The Interim Constitution represented a compromise and a genuine attempt to meet the demands of as many groups as possible. The ANC dropped its socialist dogma and tried to appeal to the White business community. They also emphasised their commitment to democracy for all South Africans, Black and White.

THE 1994 ELECTION CAMPAIGN

The ANC manifesto was entitled 'A Better Life for All'. In it they made the following pledges:

ACTIVITIES

1 What were the CODESA talks and the MPNF?
2 Describe the main features of the Interim Constitution. Remember that the Interim Constitution was to apply only from 1994 until 1999.
3 Which six parties were most important in South Africa in the lead up to the 1994 elections?

ACTIVITY

Compare the policies of the main political parties during the 1994 General Election campaign:
◆ ANC
◆ National Party
◆ Inkatha Freedom Party
◆ Freedom Front
◆ Democratic Party
◆ Pan African Congress

◆ Employment and training for an additional 2.5 million people in five years.
◆ Government support for small businesses.
◆ Government support for workers' rights and Trade Unions.
◆ Provision of a million homes with running water and toilets.
◆ Improved health care and immunisation programmes.
◆ Increased public expenditure financed by economic growth.

The National Party tried to win support for all races with the following main points in their Manifesto:
◆ They had been responsible for ending apartheid.
◆ They had the necessary experience and credibility to govern.
◆ They would implement radical measures to create jobs, build houses and improve health care
◆ The ANC had dangerous links with the South African Communist Party.

The Inkatha Freedom Party initially refused to take part in the elections, saying that the constitutional format had been rigged by the ANC. However, as the move towards democracy gathered pace the IFP could not stay outside mainstream politics, and just one week before the election they agreed to put up candidates. Inkatha's main aim had always been to establish an independent Zulu state outside of South Africa, based around their population base in Natal. At the 1994 election they stood on a ticket of strengthening the powers of the provincial assemblies, to gain more autonomy for the Natal Assembly. During the fighting between ANC supporters and Inkatha in 1994/5, it is estimated that some 13 500 people died. When they did agree to put up candidates the main concession made by the ANC was to allow the Zulu Royal Family to remain nominal leaders in the Natal province.

The Afrikaner Volksfront (AVF) really wanted to create a separate Afrikaner state, in the same way as Inkatha wanted an independent Zulu state. However, like Inkatha, the AVF compromised for the 1994 elections and looked for increased power to be given to the provinces. The ANC and the National Party made some concessions to the AVF, giving the provinces increased tax-raising powers and the right to determine their own government structure. Together with some of the more extreme right-wing groups, the AVF formed the Freedom Front. The credibility of the far right was shattered when the AWB, led by the volatile Eugene Terreblanche, mounted an armed assault on Black civilians in the homeland of Boputhatswana. Media coverage of the event, which showed atrocities in graphic detail, forced the Freedom Front to adopt a wholly peaceful approach. The Afrikaner right was split – some chose to support the democratic process and voted for the Freedom Front – others boycotted the election completely. The result was that the influence of the noisy and dangerous extremists was diluted.

POST-APARTHEID SOUTH AFRICA

In this chapter you will learn about:
- ◆ free elections in South Africa
- ◆ economic and social problems facing South Africa
- ◆ government in South Africa after Nelson Mandela
- ◆ crime and punishment in South Africa

South Africans voting in free democratic elections in 1994

1994 GENERAL ELECTION RESULT

Voting took place between April 26th and 28th – the poll had to be extended for a day to accommodate all those who wished to take part. Although there were some hitches with polling stations running out of ballot papers, and accusations that election agents were 'coaching' people on whom to vote for, the Independent Electoral Commission was pleased with the way the election was conducted. Fears of large-scale violence proved to be unfounded.

The result gave the ANC a majority to dominate the new government, but they did not reach the magic two-thirds figure which would have allowed them to alter the interim constitution without reference to other parties. The National Party crossed the 20% threshold to ensure that they would have a post of Vice President which acted to reassure the whites. It is notable that the National Party received over 20% of the votes yet Whites make up only 15% of the population – the extra votes came mainly from Indians and Coloureds.

The Inkatha Freedom Party achieved a half-share of the votes in Natal province, and their strength in the new Parliament meant that they had three Cabinet posts. The Freedom Front succeeded in bringing many Afrikaners into the democratic process. Only the AWB mounted a serious terrorist threat to the election, with the majority of Afrikaners content to support the Freedom Front or simply abstain from the vote completely.

THE RESULT

Votes Counted:	19 726 579
Percentage Poll:	86.9%
Spoilt Papers:	193 081
Percentage Spoilt:	0.99%
Votes Accepted:	19 533 497

Party	Votes	%	Seats
African National Congress	12 237 655	62.65	252
National Party	3 983 690	20.39	82
Inkatha Freedom Party	2 058 294	10.54	43
Freedom Front	424 555	2.17	9
Democratic Party	338 426	1.73	7
Pan African Congress	243 478	1.25	5
African Christian Democratic Party	88 104	0.45	2
African Muslim Party	34 466	0.18	
African Moderates Congress Party	27 690	0.14	
Dikwankwetla Party	19 451	0.10	
Federal Party	17 663	0.09	
Minority Party	13 433	0.07	
Soccer Party	10 575	0.05	
African Democratic Movement	9886	0.05	
Women's Rights Peace Party	6434	0.04	
Ximoko Progressive Party	6320	0.03	
Keep It Straight and Simple	5916	0.03	
Workers List Party	4169	0.02	
Luso South African Party	3292	0.02	

Previous negotiations between the parties had resulted in the concept of a 'Government of National Unity' where all major political groups would take part in the governing of the new South Africa. These provisions were set out in the Interim Constitution. The philosophy behind these arrangements was designed to bring about reconciliation between the previously bitterly divided racial groups and to calm White fears about a Black dominated 'Communist' ANC government.

The leader of the government was Nelson Mandela, leader of the ANC. He selected two Deputy presidents to assist him in the task of rebuilding South Africa. His right-hand man became FW De Klerk, who was described by Mandela as:

'One of the greatest reformers, one of the greatest sons of our soil.'

The other Deputy President was Thabo Mbeki, the Deputy Leader of the ANC. Mandela knew the difficulties that were ahead and the agony and bitterness of the past. His main task alongside building a just society was to create a spirit of reconciliation rather than one of revenge. In his first speech as President he said:

'Out of the experiences of an extraordinary human disaster that lasted too long must be born a society of which all humanity can be proud.'

Mandela had a difficult task. Not only did he have to win the confidence of the White and Zulu communities, neither of which had supported the ANC, he also had to involve those on the left of the ANC who stood by the original Freedom Charter and its talk of nationalising industry, redistributing land, wealth and power. The need for 'balance' was highlighted by the composition of Mandela's first Cabinet. Out of loyalty to his old comrades in the Freedom Front, Mandela gave three Cabinet posts to the 'old left'. Trade Union leader Jay Naidoo (Reconstruction and Development), Communist Party leader Joe Slovo (Housing), and ANC guerrilla leader Joe Modise (Defence) were all given Cabinet appointments. The remainder of the Cabinet posts reflected a range of views within the ANC, the National Party and Inkatha – Chief Buthelezi was made Home Affairs minister.

ACTIVITIES

1 Describe the results of the 1994 general Election.
2 Why could the election be said to be a very fair reflection of the views of the people?
3 Under the terms of the Interim Constitution, which parties were involved in the 'government of national unity'?

SOUTH AFRICA'S NEW CONSTITUTION

South Africa's political system contains a written Bill of Rights. This is a document which sets out the rights of every South African. In particular, it says that no person should be discriminated against on the grounds of gender, race, religion, disability, culture, language or sexual orientation.

The South African Parliament has two chambers. The National Assembly is elected every five years. The National Council of the Provinces acts as the 'upper chamber' of Parliament. Each province sends a delegation of ten people, which casts one vote on behalf of their province. The National Council of the the Provinces can stop legislation, which must then go back to the National Assembly and receive a two-third majority to go through. The ANC are close to the two-thirds level, but cannot guarantee to get all legislation past the National Council of the Provinces.

The provinces of South Africa have been given control over a range of policy areas. These include education (not universities), health services and housing. Some of the provincial governments – notably in KwaZulu Natal and Western Cape, where the ANC are less powerful – argue that too much power is given to central government and not enough to the provinces. The Inkatha Freedom Party, from its stronghold in KwaZulu Natal, has demanded a full Federal system, with maximum powers being devolved to the provinces.

THE RECONSTRUCTION AND DEVELOPMENT PLAN (RDP) – ADDRESSING SOCIAL AND ECONOMIC PROBLEMS

The leaders of the new South Africa faced huge economic and social problems. The divide between the mainly rich White population, and the almost entirely poor Black population was huge. Average figures for housing standards, educational achievement, income etc. do not reveal the true picture – it is necessary to look at figures broken down by racial group.

Indicator	Average monthly household income (Rand)	Professional or Managerial Employees (%)	Maximum monthly Social Pensions (Rand)	Infant deaths per 1000 live births (1988)
Blacks	352	0.31	149.7	62
Whites	1958	26.56	250.7	9
Coloureds	680	1.17	199.7	41
Asians	1109	3.45	199.7	14
W:B	5.59	86.68	1.67	0.15

Indicator	Unemployment Rates (1994)		Incidence of tuberculosis (per 100 000 population)	Expenditure on school pupils per capita (Rand)	Pupils per Teacher
	Male	Female			
Blacks	34%	50%	164	595	41
Coloureds	20%	28%	532	1508	25
Asians	13%	24%	53	2015	20
Whites	5%	9%	16	2722	16
W:B	0.14%	0.18%	0.10	4.57	0.39

Access to Services, By Population Group (%) – 1994

	Black	White	Coloured	Asian
Refuse collection	80	100	98	98
Toilet	34	100	83	97
Mains Water	31	100	76	99
Tap Water	27	98	76	98
Telephone	12	87	43	72

Access to Services for Black South Africans (%) – 1994

	Urban	Rural
Tap Water	86	29
Refuse Collection	80	5
Flush Toilet	72	7
Mains Electricity	58	11
Telephone	25	2

It is also important to note how the composition of South Africa's population had changed over a period of time.

Percentage of Population

Year	Blacks	Whites	Asians	Coloureds
1960	68.3	19.3	3.0	9.4
1970	70.4	17.3	2.9	9.4
1980	72.5	15.6	2.9	9.0
1988	74.9	13.8	2.6	8.7

ACTIVITIES

1 Using the figures provided, write a 150-word summary of the economic and social problems faced by South Africa in 1994.

2 How had the composition of the South African population altered over time?

3 Identify the main economic, housing, health and education priorities for South Africa.

4 Describe the six principles of the RDP.

5 What were the five key programmes of the RDP?

6 List some of the targets set in the RDP.

Remember that the phrase RDP is no longer used. The aims and targets remain the same, but they are now the responsibility of different government departments, rather than a separate RDP Office.

SUMMARY OF THE CHALLENGES THAT MANDELA'S FIRST GOVERNMENT FACED

At the outset the Reconstruction and Development Programme (RDP) had massive problems to address. These are summarised below.

The Economy

◆ During the early 1990s the South African economy suffered a severe recession – in 1992, for example, the economy contracted by 2%. This was due to the lingering effects of sanctions and a lack of competitiveness.

◆ Under Mandela the decline in foreign investment was reversed and South African business gained better access to foreign markets due to world reaction to the democratisation of the country. The South African economy grew by over 2% in 1995.

◆ This level of growth was unlikely to create a huge reduction in inequality in the short term, as the problems facing South Africa were so severe. In 1994 for instance:

◆ 46% of the workforce were unemployed

◆ 2.8% annual increase in workforce

◆ 9 million South Africans were destitute

◆ 10 million lacked access to running water

◆ 21 million had inadequate sanitation

◆ 23 million had no access to electricity.

The economy would need to grow by 4% each year just to stop unemployment from rising.

◆ Despite the fact that foreign investors pumped $5 billion into South Africa between 1994 and 1996, the situation was still worsening.

Housing

Under apartheid all Africans living in urban settlements were considered to be there temporarily. This meant only limited efforts were made to improve conditions in the townships. Only 5000 houses were provided for Black Africans in urban areas during the whole of the 1970s. The consequence of such neglect was that 300 000 houses per year had to be built for the foreseeable future to deal with the housing shortage.

Health Care

Current inequalities mean that life expectancy for Whites is 73 years, for Africans 63 years. Infant mortality rates for Whites are 7 per 1000, and for Africans 52 per 1000.

Also Africans have grown up in an environment where violence is commonplace. Violence and the lack of opportunity have damaged the role of family life.

Education

- The literacy rate amongst South African Blacks is only around 50% – this is less than in neighbouring Black African countries which are poorer than South Africa.
- Under Apartheid most Africans were taught in their native language for the first six years, reducing their chance of being able to read and write English.
- Provision of education facilities at all levels was segregated. This resulted in inferior provision for non-Whites of all abilities.
- '*No education before liberation*' was a slogan of the apartheid years. The actions of young Africans were significant in bringing down apartheid. School boycotts and the appeal of protesting rather than learning means that South Africa has a 'lost generation' of people who are not as well educated as they might be.
- More than half of all African pupils drop out of school after just seven years.
- Only 16% of Africans entering school finish their studies compared to 85% of whites.
- A study in 1992 showed that 1.7 million African people between six and seventeen do not attend school.

During the 1994 election campaign, and then in government, the ANC made various promises about what they would do to improve social and economic conditions. The RDP was the policy designed to bring these promises to reality. The government knew that the Black voters expected a rapid transformation in their lives. They had put their faith in Mandela and peaceful change, rather than continuing the armed struggle. However, Mandela knew that any rapid redistribution of wealth from White to Black would destroy the business community, and wipe out jobs. Foreign investment would also be scared away. The RDP had to be a juggling act to try and keep all sides happy.

The RDP covered far more than just economic development, envisaging nothing less than the transformation of an entire society – the way it thinks as well as the way it operates. All the main political parties support the broad aims of the RDP.

The total cost of the RDP was estimated at $15–25 billion. The main items of expenditure were planned to be social services (26%), education and training (22%), housing (18%), water and sanitation (13%) and rural development (12%). The money required for the RDP was to come from:

- foreign investment
- national lottery
- budget re-allocations from other departments
- sale of state-owned assets.

The RDP was based on six fundamental principles:

- Integration and sustainability – the legacy of apartheid could not be overcome with piecemeal, uncoordinated policies. The programme had to be affordable and sustainable. Strong central government and financial discipline were central to this.

◆ People driven approach – development is not about the delivery of goods to a passive population. It must involve the people. People have to be taught about taking more responsibility for improving their own lives.

◆ Peace and security – the endemic violence faced by communities in South Africa had to be combated, with special attention to the various forms of violence to which women were subjected. The aim was to establish neutral security forces with a demilitarised ethic. Decisive action was required to tackle lawlessness, drug trafficking, gun-running, fraud, and the abuse of women and children. Crime had become a major political issue.

◆ Nation building – national sovereignty had to be consolidated on the basis of 'unity in diversity'.

◆ Meeting basic needs and building the infrastructure – the provision of better telecommunications, transport, housing, electricity and education was seen as central to the development of the country.

◆ Democratisation – democracy was to be seen as a continuous process, not just a one-off at elections. People must be accountable and accessible for the decisions that they make.

Within the RDP there were five key programmes:

◆ *Meeting Basic Needs*. Providing jobs, land reform, water, sanitation, energy, nutrition, health care etc. identified special 'presidential projects' in the areas of greatest need.

◆ *Developing Human Resources*. If education and training was made available to everyone regardless of race, age and gender, then the full potential of the population could be realised.

◆ *Building the Economy*. The wealth accrued from South Africa's mining needed to be spread more evenly across the country instead of being concentrated with the wealthy few. However, the government backed away from a policy of nationalisation, and has actually privatised some state-owned assets.

◆ *Democratising the State and Society*. The civil service, law enforcement authorities and government were rife with corruption. The aim was to build a public service that was not tainted in any way. The Truth Commission was established to try and uncover some of the secrets from the past, without prosecuting those implicated.

◆ *Implementing the RDP*. Extensive consultation was to take place before implementation. Some of the first targets set by the government were ambitious. By setting such high expectations, they were in a sense setting themselves up to be accused of failure should they fail to meet them.

The targets included:

◆ Building one million low-cost homes by 1999.
◆ Redistributing 30% of land within five years.

◆ Introducing compulsory ten-year education, with class sizes restricted to a maximum of 40 by the year 2000.

◆ Providing all schools and 2.5 million homes with electricity.

◆ Creating 300 000 – 500 000 jobs per annum within five years.

◆ Providing immediate free health care to all children under six and pregnant women.

◆ Giving a free 'Mandela Sandwich' each day to five million primary school children in over 12 000 schools.

◆ Providing water and sanitation for 169 villages and 411 000 people.

◆ Undertaking urban renewal projects in four major black townships.

Extracts from a Government publication about the RDP illustrate the sort of problems it was designed to address:

'Our townships have for too long been characterised by sewage flowing in the streets, rubbish heaped by the roadside, potholed roads, no electricity, broken telephones, burned out community centres, sub-standard crowded dwellings and ineffective and illegitimate local government... Since the Free Health Care Programme started, no child under six years of age and no pregnant woman may be turned away from a hospital or clinic ... 172 new clinics will be built through the Clinic Building Programme by April 1996... South Africa needs a culture of learning. This programme will put education back on its feet. Broader change in education must address low attendance, poor exam results and the breakdown of discipline, by tackling the root causes including resource shortage, teacher training and education management.'

The RDP met with limited success. Some of the specific targets which were set down were not achieved, mainly for economic reasons. The South African government simply could not afford to spend the amount of money that would have been necessary to effect such progress in the short term.

The lack of success brought a mixed response from Black South Africans. Some were content that the government was now in their hands, and understood that changes would take a long time to happen. Others believed that rapid change was required and became impatient with the ANC leaders, and prefered to see a much more radical approach adopted.

At the 1997 National Conference of the ANC Nelson Mandela re-stated the core values of the RDP. He admitted that some of the targets would not be met, but that the philosophy of the RDP should continue to underlie government policy in social and economic areas.

Mandela was convinced that it was necessary to maintain the basic business and commercial infrastructure as it was in the apartheid period. To totally dismantle the system and transfer all the business and wealth to the Blacks would not make any sense. Investment would end, unemployment would rise, and conditions would deteriorate. Even spreading the wealth equally around all the people of the country would simply leave everyone poor. Mandela's loyal supporters accepted his approach – and the self-restraint required to adopt such a conciliatory and dignified position after suffering so much was an indication of the stature of the man and his party. However, the longer the country goes without seeing really significant economic progress, then the more difficult it will be for the ANC leadership to justify their position.

Late in 1996 the RDP was scrapped. Although the aims and policies remained much the same, the separate RDP Office was closed, and they were now integrated into the work of other government departments and provincial governments.

The South African government published a new plan known as the Growth, Employment and Redistribution Strategy (GEAR). This recognised the fact that the targets set out in the RDP were not being met, because the underlying economic conditions were not right. Consequently, GEAR aimed to:

◆ keep a tight control on government spending
◆ attract foreign investment into South Africa
◆ make Trade Unions accept lower wage increases
◆ reduce trade tariffs to make South Africa's products more attractive
◆ privatise some state-owned industries such as telecommunications, electricity and the airlines

In simple terms GEAR aimed to create the economic growth that would allow the RDP targets to be met. Economic growth means that the amount of money in the economy is increasing. Individuals will have more to spend – creating jobs. The government will take more in taxes – allowing them to spend more. Economic growth is the key to modernising South Africa.

ECONOMIC AND SOCIAL CONDITIONS IN THE NEW MILLENNIUM

As South Africa entered the new millennium, experts looked back at the progress that had been made since the election of the first multi-racial government in 1994.

Despite strenuous efforts, South Africa's economy was still struggling. Economic growth was not fast enough to generate the wealth necessary to address many of the problems of the country. Foreign investment was less than expected. This was really a 'chicken and egg' situation. Foreign investors did not want to put their money into South Africa until the population were better off and therefore provided a good market. The people would not become better off until foreign investment increased.

Unemployment was still a massive problem in South Africa. Accurate figures are difficult to obtain, but most estimates said that the employment situation was little better than it had been in 1994. Many Africans were employed illegally and unofficially, and therefore paid no taxes.

Good progress had been made in housing. Around 400 000 new houses had been built in the six years from 1994 to 2000. Many townships had been provided with electricity and water supplies. In total more than five million homes had been provided with electricity – getting people to pay their bills was another matter! Many people risked electrocution by illegally tapping into electricity supplies by running their own cables to sub-stations and switch boxes.

Primary health care was an important part of the RDP and GEAR. Many new Primary Health Centres were built, and programmes of immunisation against diseases like polio were successful. More than five million children each day benefited from the 'Mandela Sandwich'.

In education, provision for Africans still lags way behind that for Whites. There is an in-built opposition to education in some quarters. This dates from the years of school boycotts, and also from the need for children to earn a living at as early an age as possible to supplement family income.

The issue of land reform has been important. Landless peasants were promised the chance to buy land. However, landowners have been guaranteed that they will get the market price of their land. The result has been that fewer than half-a-million poor South Africans have been able to buy land. They are given a grant of 15 000 Rands, but this is simply not enough.

ACTIVITY

Compile a report on the economic and social progress made in South Africa during the 1990s.

Use the following headlines:
- economic and social conditions during the apartheid period
- the aims of the RDP
- the work of the RDP
- how successful was the RDP?
- the GEAR programme

AFFIRMATIVE ACTION OR NOT?

Affirmative Action means positive discrimination. Groups that have been the victims of discrimination in the past can be given favourable treatment in the future to make-up for the unfair treatment. Affirmative Action was used in the United States of America from the 1960s onwards to compensate for the discrimination in employment suffered by Black Americans. The issue of Affirmative Action in South Africa is controversial.

The most high-profile examples of Affirmative Action involve high-level jobs such as administration in the public sector. In government departments the top civil servants were almost exclusively White. They have been offered redundancy packages to try to get them to leave, so that their jobs can be advertised again and a better balance of ethnic groups appointed. In some cases officials have been removed from their top posts to more junior jobs, and given a conserved salary.

Affirmative action is not popular with White South Africans. They see it as a form of 'tokenism'. *'Incompetent people can end up being promoted far beyond their abilities,'* said one opponent. Some White professionals would rather leave South Africa than end up losing out in the employment-market due to affirmative action.

ACTIVITY

Explain clearly what is meant by Affirmative Action.
Using South Africa as an example, do you think that a policy of Affirmative Action is justified?

Chief Buthelezi

POLITICAL DEVELOPMENTS SINCE 1994

The Inkatha Freedom Party and Chief Buthelezi are campaigning for the formation of an autonomous KwaZulu/Natal province – a Zulu Kingdom. Buthelezi encouraged his supporters to 'rise and resist' after the 1994 elections, and since then several thousand people have been killed in violence between Inkatha and ANC supporters. The ANC are firmly against Buthelezi's demands for greater autonomy in Natal – they believe that the federal structure of the constitution gives ample independence to the regions. They feel that Buthelezi is simply trying to regain some of the power and status he enjoyed under the apartheid regime, when he was courted by the White government as an opponent of the ANC. When the final constitution for the country, to be implemented after 1999, was written in 1996 the IFP again agitated for greater power to the provinces. They were thwarted on that occasion, but the problem will not go away.

Within the ANC there have been growing demands from the left of the party for a more radical stance on social and economic policies. Embarrassingly for President Mandela, one of the most prominent voices was that of his ex-wife Winnie Mandela, who had long been a favourite with the radical young groups within the ANC. She stated that 'reconciliation with the Whites is an act of indulgence which the Blacks cannot afford'.

The question of a successor to Mandela was settled late in 1997. His Deputy as leader of the ANC, Thabo Mbeki, was named as the 'heir apparent' to assume control when Mandela stepped down at the time of the 1999 elections. Mbeki's background is from the far left, but showed little sign of leftist tendencies during his spell as Deputy President. However, with Mandela gone after 1999, Mbeki had a hard choice to make in choosing which path to follow. Should he continue the avenue opened by Mandela and try to appease the Whites and attempt further reconciliation? Or should he listen to the voices of the more radical Blacks and move away from the vision of a multi-racial South Africa and switch to a Black South Africa? The outcome of the 1999 election gave the ANC an overall majority, and gave them a mandate to implement whatever policies they wanted.

ACTIVITIES

1   What is the main aim for the Inkatha Freedom Party?
2   What evidence is there of division within the ANC?
3   What difficult choice faces President Thabo Mbeki?

TRUTH AND RECONCILIATION COMMISSION

The Truth and Reconciliation Commission investigated crimes of murder and sabotage which occurred during the apartheid years. Many of the revelations were predictable, but not particularly significant. For example, the truth about the death of Steve Biko emerged – he died because of police brutality, not as a result of the accident that had been maintained during the years of repression. Winnie Mandela was brought before the Truth Commission to answer allegations about her activities and those of her group of

Winnie Mandela

bodyguards – the Mandela United Football Club – whilst her husband was in prison. She was accused of ordering the murder of several ANC moderates, but in her testimony to the Commission she denied everything. As the Commission was not a court as such – it merely offers people the chance to tell the truth about what happened in the past – it was not possible to examine these incidents further.

Other 'truths' that emerged included:

◆ White scientists had worked on a bacteria that would only kill Black people.
◆ Government ministers had ordered the bombing of any cinema that showed the film 'Cry Freedom', about the life of Steve Biko.
◆ Government had ordered the bombing of the headquarters of the South African Council of Churches.

Although the TRC was helpful in revealing the truth about things that had happened in South Africa, it was criticised for not doing more. The people who ordered killings and bombings during the apartheid era never appeared before the Commission. One member of the secret police force stated that his orders had come from the very top. Former President PW Botha, leader of South Africa in the late 70s and early 80s, refused to testify to the Commission.

The fighting between the ANC and Inkatha was never fully investigated, despite horrendous violence and brutality that took place. Critics said that the ANC's image would have suffered if the truth came out.

The TRC never investigated the links between the White National Party and the Inkatha Freedom Party. It was often suggested that the White government were behind many of the atrocities in the feud between Inkatha and the ANC, with the aim of de-stabilising the country and defeating the ANC.

THE NEW NATIONAL PARTY

The National Party, led by De Klerk at the time of the 1994 elections, also underwent substantial changes. They withdrew from the Government of National Unity in 1996 in order to make full and proper preparations for the 1999 General Election, which were fought on partisan lines. De Klerk resigned as Vice President of South Africa and the National Party members of the Cabinet also left their posts. They knew that there would be no 'government of national unity' after the 1999 election – the biggest party would assume absolute control of the country, if they had more than 50% of the representatives in Parliament. In September 1997 De Klerk stepped down as leader of the party, saying that he was too closely linked with the apartheid period, and that the party should have a new leader for the multi-racial era. Support for the National Party fell in the wake of his decision.

ACTIVITIES

1 What was the purpose of the Truth and Reconciliation Commission?
2 What were some of the 'truths' that emerged?
3 Why was it unfortunate that PW Botha would not testify to the Commission?
4 Why do you think that the feud between the ANC and Inkatha was never fully investigated?

The party changed its name to the New National Party but support fell from 20% in 1994 to just 7% in 1999. Obviously many Whites felt that the new National Party was toothless as an opposition to the ANC, and they may not have voted at all. Others switched to the Democratic Party which became the biggest of the White political groups.

ACTIVITIES

1 Why did the National Party withdraw from the Government of National Unity in 1996?
2 What happened to support for the National Party after this?

PROFILE – NELSON MANDELA

1918	Born in the Eastern Cape, son of a tribal chief
1944	Formed the Youth League of the African National Congress, with close friends Walter Sisulu and Oliver Tambo
1956	Charged with high treason by South African government
1958	Married Winnie
1961	Acquitted on charges of high treason
1964	Sentenced to life imprisonment on charges of sabotage and treason
1990	Freed from prison after 27 years
1994	Elected President after the first multi-racial elections in South Africa
1998	Marries his third wife, on his 80th birthday
1999	Steps down as leader of the ANC and President of South Africa

ACTIVITY

Write a report on the political career of Nelson Mandela. Mention his qualities that made him such a successful politician.

1999 GENERAL ELECTION RESULTS

The table on the opposite page shows the results of the 1999 General Election for the National Assembly. This was the first election to be fought on a 'winner takes all' basis. The only party with a chance of taking over 50% of the seats was the ANC – which they duly achieved.

Party	Seats	Percent
African Christian Democratic Party (ACDP)	6	1.43
African National Congress (ANC)	266	66.35
Afrikaner Eenheids Beweging (AEB)	1	0.29
Azanian People's Organisation (AZAPO)	1	0.17
Democratic Party (DP)	38	9.56
Federal Alliance (FA)	2	0.54
Inkatha Freedom Party (IFP)	34	8.58
Minority Front (MF)	1	0.30
New National Party (NNP)	28	6.87
Pan Africanist Congress of Azania (PAC)	3	0.71
Green Party (GP)	0	0.06
Socialist Party of Azania (SOPA)	0	0.06
United Christian Democratic Party (UCDP)	3	0.78
United Democratic Movement (UDM)	14	3.42
Freedom Front (FF)	3	0.80
Abolition of Income Tax Party (AITUP)	0	0.07

15 977 026 people cast their votes giving a turnout of 89.3 per cent.

REGIONAL ELECTION RESULTS

At the same time as the General Election, voters also elected Provincial Assemblies for each of the nine provinces. These results show clearly that the support for each party tends to be concentrated in particular regions. The exception to this is the ANC which has widespread support throughout the country.

Party	Eastern Cape	Free State	Gauteng	Kwazulu-Natal	Mpumalanga	Northern Cape	Northern Province	North-West	Western Cape
ANC	47	25	50	32	26	20	44	27	18
DP	4	2	13	7	1	1	1	1	5
NNP	2	2	3	3	1	8	1	1	17
PAC	1	–	–	–	–	–	1	–	–
UCDP	–	–	–	–	–	–	–	3	–
UDM	9	–	1	1	1	–	1	–	1
FF	–	1	1	–	1	1	–	1	–
ACDP	–	–	1	1	–	–	1	–	1
FA	–	–	1	–	–	–	–	–	–
IFP	–	–	3	34	–	–	–	–	–
MF	–	–	–	2	–	–	–	–	–

ACTIVITIES

Compare the performance of the following political parties in each of the provinces of South Africa:

◆ ANC
◆ Inkatha
◆ Democratic Party
◆ New National Party
◆ United Christian Democratic Party
◆ United Democratic Movement
◆ Freedom Front

President Thabo Mbeki

PROFILE – THABO MVUYELWA MBEKI PRESIDENT OF THE REPUBLIC OF SOUTH AFRICA

Personal

◆ Date of birth: 18 June 1942, Idutywa, Queenstown, one of four children of Govan and Epainette Mbeki
◆ Marital status: Married to Zanele Dlamini (1974)

Academic Qualifications

◆ Attended primary school in Idutywa and Butterworth
◆ Acquired high school education at Lovedale, Alice
◆ Expelled from school as a result of student strikes (1959) and forced to continue studies at home
◆ Completed British A level examinations (1960 and 1961)
◆ Undertook first year economics degree on a correspondence course with the University of London (1961–1962)
◆ Master of Economics degree, University of Sussex (1966)

Career/Memberships/Positions/Other Activities

◆ Joined ANC Youth League (ANCYL) while a student at Lovedale Institute (1956)
◆ Involved in underground activities in the Pretoria-Witwatersrand area after the ANC was banned in 1960
◆ Involved in mobilising the students and youth in support of the ANC call for a stay at home in protest against the creation of a Republic (1961)
◆ Elected Secretary of the African Students Association (December 1961)
◆ Left South Africa together with other students on instructions of the ANC (1962). Went to the then Southern Rhodesia (now Zimbabwe), the then Tanganyika (now Tanzania) and the United Kingdom to study
◆ Continued with political activities as a university student in the UK, mobilising the international student community against apartheid
◆ Worked for the ANC office in London (1967 – 1970). Underwent military training in the then Soviet Union during this period
◆ Served as Assistant Secretary to the Revolutionary Council of the ANC in Lusaka (1971)
◆ Sent to Botswana (1973). He was among the first ANC leaders to have contact with exiled and visiting members of the Black Consciousness Movement (BCM). As a result of his contact and discussions with the BCM, some of the leading members of this organisation found their way into the ranks of the ANC
◆ Director of the Department of Information and Publicity (1984 – 1989)
◆ Re-elected to the NEC (1985). Served as Director of Information and as Secretary for Presidential Affairs
◆ Member of the ANC's political and military council

♦ Member of the delegation that met the South African business community led by the Chairman of Anglo American, Gavin Relly, at Mfuwe, Zambia (1985)
♦ Led a delegation of the ANC to Dakar, Senegal, where talks were held with a delegation from the Institute for a Democratic Alternative for South Africa (Idasa) (1987)
♦ Led the ANC delegation which held secret talks with the South African government from 1989 and which led to agreements about the unbanning of the ANC and the release of political prisoners
♦ Participated in negotiations leading to the adoption of the interim Constitution for the new South Africa
♦ Elected chairperson of the ANC (1993). The election to this post meant succeeding the late former President and chairperson of the ANC, OR Tambo, with whom he has had a close working relationship over the years
♦ Executive Deputy President in the South African Government (since 1994)

Current positions:
♦ President of the Republic of South Africa (since 14 June 1999)
♦ President of the ANC (since 1997)

ACTIVITY

Imagine that you have been asked to write a 100-word report summarising the main achievements on Thabo Mbeki. Try to include as much information as possible in your report, while sticking to the word limit.

CASE STUDY

Crime in South Africa

The level of crime in South Africa gives real cause for concern – the government is clearly unable to uphold the rule of law. The murder rate in South Africa is seven times that of the United States. In the first nine months of 1997 an average of 67 people were murdered every day. Car-jacking, where people are stopped on the roads at gun point, is common. Their cars are stolen and usually they are shot dead.

Much of the crime is organised by criminal gangs, and some believe that former security staff and police officers are heavily involved. Some of the crime may be meant to destabilise the country and cause a situation of anarchy to arise, leading to the fall of the government.

Crime reports from the South African press

All the reports below appeared in the South African press between October 14th and 20th 1999. There were literally hundreds of other crime reports – these are just a small sample!

Girl raped in farm attack on East Rand

Johannesburg – A 12-year-old girl was raped in her farmhouse near Nigel on Tuesday when four men held her, her brother and her grandmother up, according to an East Rand police report. Police said the attackers took the girl into her bedroom and raped her. Her brother and grandmother were tied up in the lounge. Police later arrested one man after the East Rand highway patrol spotted a vehicle stolen from the farm in Duduza. 'The car seemed abandoned and one of the members went to investigate, not knowing that the driver of the vehicle was standing in a group of people nearby pointing a firearm at him,' said a police spokeswoman Inspector Alet de Vos. Another policeman arrested the driver, whose firearm came from the farm. Other goods stolen – a video machine and clothing – were recovered. One firearm, however, was still missing.

Country club attacked

Queenstown – Lady Grey Country Club manager Alf Pittaway suffered head injuries in an attack at the club on Friday, police said yesterday. Pittaway was locking up at 8.45pm when two men beat him with an iron bar. He activated the alarm and police arrived shortly afterwards, but the men had fled.

Two men, guard killed in Bethlehem robbery

Bloemfontein – Two robbers and a security guard were killed in a shootout in Bethlehem on Monday when four men attempted to rob a security company, Free State police said. A police spokesperson said three men approached two security guards at about 11.20am after they collected money from a business in Bethlehem. A shootout occurred and two robbers and a security guard were wounded. One of the robbers died on the scene. The second robber and the security guard died later in hospital. Police said the third man and a driver made off with a money trunk in a grey Ford Meteor. Police later recovered the vehicle, which was abandoned, and later the stolen money at a nearby house. No arrests were made.

Ninth mob-killing suspect arrested

Johannesburg – Police on Monday arrested a ninth suspect in connection with last week's death of a man suspected of raping a 16-year-old girl in Daveyton township on the East Rand. Superintendent Eugene Opperman said the suspect was believed to be part the mob that assaulted Lazaro Motla after he and an accomplice were pointed out by the victim as her attackers. Eight other suspects were arrested earlier on Sunday and are scheduled to appear in court on Tuesday.

Two armed robberies

UMTATA – Armed robbers made off with more than R19 000 in two separate incidents here yesterday. Police said two armed men robbed Way Enterprise Store in Madeira Street shortly after 1pm. A man ordered workers to lie on their stomachs while another emptied the tills. They fled on foot with R7700. An hour later armed robbers hit Bonita Butchery where they stole R12 000.

Italian tourists robbed in Johannesburg

Two Italian tourists were robbed by eight knife-wielding men while waiting for a bus in Johannesburg on Thursday, police spokesperson Captain Lungelo Dlamini said. Cash, passports, a camera and travellers' cheques were stolen from Elizabeth Ferrari and Giovanna Oppio. The eight men grabbed the women and forced them to hand over their belongings.

Hearse hijacked with body

Johannesburg – Hijackers carefully removed the body of a woman on a stretcher outside the Elka Stadium in Soweto before racing off in a hearse which they had earlier hijacked, an undertaker said yesterday. Mr Joseph Kupu was hijacked while taking the body from the Leratong Hospital to the undertakers in Koster. Three men in a Mercedes blocked the way of the hearse and forced Kupu into the boot of the car. Kupu was dumped in Diepkloof. The body was not damaged.

53439 'prisoners-in-waiting'

Cape Town – South Africa had 53 439 awaiting-trial prisoners at the end of July this year, Correctional Services Minister Ben Skosana said yesterday. This was down from a peak of 57 666 in April this year, but up from 46 342 in August last year, he said in written reply to a question from Mr Lawrence Lever of the Democratic Party.

ACTIVITIES

'Crime is a major problem in South Africa.'
– view of Konstant Thijssen
What evidence is there to support the view of Konstant Thijssen?

INDEX